MW00915914

This is a workbook to help children understand and improve mental health.

Dedicated to my nephews,

Justin and **Jared Harvey** and **Noah Ketterman**

Edited by

Dale Flanagan

A Mastering Mental Health Curriculum

www.masteringmentalhealth.com

ISBN: 978-1544867328

Version 1.0

Table of Contents

THIS PAGE INTENTIONALY LEFT BLANK.

LESSON ONE

THE MASK

WHAT ARE MASKS?

IDENTIFYING INWARD EMOTIONS

IDENTIFYING OUTWARD EXPRESSIONS

INWARD EMOTIONS VERSUS OUTWARD EXPRESSIONS

THE MASK

"All the world's a stage, and all the men and women merely players."

-- William Shakespeare's *As You Like It*

1. In your own words, write out what you think the William Shakespeare quote means.

    _____

    _____

2. Have you ever worn a mask to an event?   YES or NO If not, pretend that you have.

3. How did (would) wearing a mask make you feel?

    _____

4. Did (would) the mask make you feel more confident?   YES or NO

5. Did (would) the mask make it easier for you to be yourself?   YES or NO

6. How did (would) you feel when you took the mask off?

    _____

7. Did (would) you act different without the mask?   YES or NO

8. If so, how did (would) you act without the mask?

    _____

    _____

WHAT ARE MASKS?

We are all **actors**. We all wear emotional **masks**. Emotional masks hide our true emotions.

A **mask** is defined as something that serves to **conceal** or **disguise**. It is a pretense, a **facade** or a defense.

People have a tendency to "mask" their true feelings. Of course, an emotional mask is not a **real** object, but rather a **false** outward expression we "put on" to cover our **true** inward feelings.

Wearing a mask **hides** who we really are.

We all wear masks from time to time.

Wearing a mask, whether emotional or physical, can be a form of **self-protection**. It is a way for our true feelings to be **hidden**. It is a way to **pretend** we are someone else or a way to pretend we are feeling something different than our true feelings.

We wear masks as we play different **roles** in life. Roles such as son, daughter, spouse, student, brother, sister, aunt, uncle, friend, employee, member, or neighbor may prompt us to wear different masks.

Masks are often worn to portray a **positive** outward expression and to hide **negative** inward emotions.

(Positive) *(Negative)*

Outward Expression   **Inward Emotion**

IDENTIFYING INWARD EMOTIONS

9.   In the chart below are emoticons that represent common emotions. *Color or mark at least three emoticons to indicate the prominent inward emotions that you have hidden behind a mask at some point in your life.* In other words, <u>what emotions do you hide from others</u>? Remember, all people wear masks from time to time.

Love	Fear	Happiness	Sadness	Anger	Surprise
😍	😱	🙂	🙁	😠	😄
Relief	Gratitude	Satisfaction	Peacefulness	Adoration	Anxiety
😜	😊	🙂	😐	🤓	😟

It is common for us to wear masks in moderation. As a matter of fact, there may be circumstances when it is good to wear a mask. Wearing a mask can serve as a temporary measure of self-control. Later, when we are in the appropriate setting, we can remove the mask and deal with the hidden negative feelings.

IDENTIFYING OUTWARD EXPRESSIONS

10. In the chart below *color or mark at least three emoticons to indicate outward expressions that you predominately use to cover up an inward emotion.* In other words, <u>what emotions do you display outwardly to others when you really feel different inwardly?</u> Remember, all people wear masks from time to time.

Love	Fear	Happiness	Sadness	Anger	Surprise
😍	😱	🙂	🙁	😠	😄
Relief	Gratitude	Satisfaction	Peacefulness	Adoration	Anxiety
😜	😊	🙂	😐	🤓	😟

INWARD EMOTIONS VERSUS OUTWARD EXPRESSIONS

Suppose your name is on your school's recipient list as a student who will receive an award. One of your closest friends tells you that one of the other recipients (to be honored along with you) cheated in order to be eligible for the award. You are not sure if the information is true. But your friend told you; so you believe it to be true. You don't tell anyone what you have heard about the alleged cheater.

The time arrives for the awards to be distributed. There is a crowd of parents, teachers, students, and administrators watching.

 Your name is called. You are presented the Second Place Award. On stage you shake hands, smile, and say "Thank You". As you walk off the stage, you hear the name of the First Place Award winner announced. It is the person who you were told had cheated. Your heart races as you think, "I should have received first place!" You stumble off the stage on your way back to your seat.

At the end of the event, family and friends approach you to offer congratulations on your Second Place Award.

11. What inward emotions do you feel?

_____

12. As you greet your family and friends, what is your outward expression? What words do you say?

_____

_____

13. What thoughts do you have about the situation?

_____

_____

LESSON TWO

ROLES – WHO AM I?

ROLE MAPPING

REVIEW – Fill in the Blanks

- A mask is defined as something that _____ or _____ .
- Wearing a mask can give a false _____ impression to cover _____ feelings.
- Masks are a form of _____-_____ .

ROLES - WHO AM I?

1. Read the following poem.

THE MASK I WEAR

Don't be fooled by me.
Don't be fooled by the face I wear
 for I wear a mask. I wear a thousand masks-
  masks that I'm afraid to take off
 and none of them are me.
Pretending is an art that's second nature with me
But don't be fooled, for God's sake, don't be fooled.
I give you the impression that I'm secure
That all is sunny and unruffled with me
 within as well as without,
  that confidence is my name
  and coolness my game,
   that the water's calm
   and I'm in command,
  and that I need no one.
But don't believe me. *Please!*   *--Author Unknown*

2. Copy the line of the poem that best describes you.

_____

Life is like a **play**. We are all **actors**! If you are asked, "Who are you?"
You may say, "I'm a sister to Ethan," or "I'm a basketball player," or
"I'm a student at Valley High School." But these things are not who you

are. These are the **roles** you **play** in life.   Remember William Shakespeare's *As You Like It*? *"All*

the world's a stage, and all the men and women merely players."

We wear different masks as we play different life roles. There are four **power** roles that we all have in life. They are <u>Family</u>, <u>Friend</u>, <u>Peer</u>, and <u>Other</u>. These power roles have sub-roles such as son, daughter, student, brother, sibling, sister, nephew, niece, aunt, uncle, close friend, student, teacher, babysitter, sports player, band member, club member, grandchild, caretaker, employee, member, or neighbor. Each role or sub-role may prompt us to wear a different mask at times.

3.   Using the list above and adding to it from your own experience, list the roles and sub-roles.

_____

_____

Often we associate people with their roles. For example, think of your favorite TV or movie star. If you should see the actress who plays your favorite character, you might associate her TV role with her as a person. But that's not who she really is. Likewise, roles have varying degrees and purposes for us. Even though some roles are prominent, it takes all the roles to make the finished product.

Imagine that you:

    A.   Are playing in a star role in an hour-long TV show.

    B.   Have a role in a 30-second commercial where you are seen for a very short time.

    C.   Are an extra in a movie.

    D.   Have no role in a TV show, commercial, or movie.

4.   Find the letter A in the graphic. The letter A is associated with A above (star role). Using the remaining examples from above, place the corresponding letters B, C, and D on the graphic to indicate where each supporting role is in relation to the prominent center star role (A).

ROLE MAPPING

Role mapping is making a diagram showing a high level overview. It helps you identify how you are connected to other people and the roles that you play in their lives. Role mapping clearly shows your relationship to others and how much power they can have on your life.

Below is an example of a role map. In this example, the person is a daughter, sister, niece, and an aunt to her family. She is a girlfriend to three people, and she has peers to whom she is a classmate, band member, and basketball player. She is an employee, student, neighbor, and a caretaker in other people's lives.

5. On the blank lines in the four power role circles, write the first name of the person (one for each power role) who has been predominant in your life in the represented role.

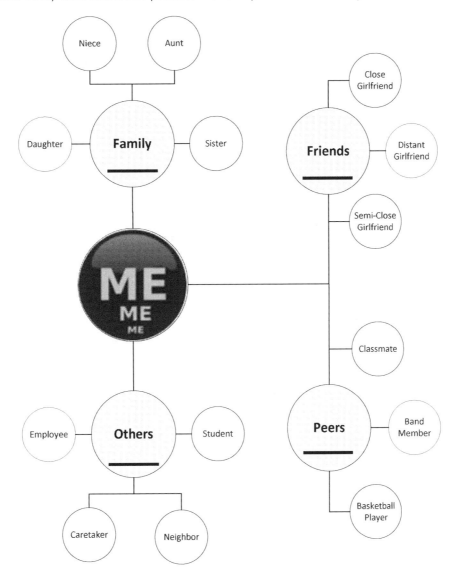

6. In the blank diagram below, write your name on each blank line representing YOU in each power role. Then fill in the sub-roles that YOU play in life as a family member, as a friend (close, semi-close, distant), as a peer, and in other roles. Add more circles, if needed.

Examples of your sub-roles may include: son, daughter, student, brother, sibling, sister, nephew, niece, aunt, uncle, close friend, student, teacher, babysitter, sports player, band member, club member, grandchild, caretaker, employee, member, or neighbor.

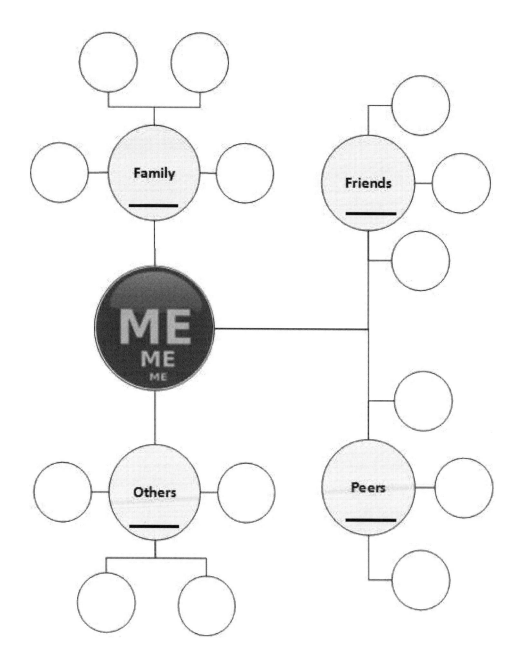

LESSON THREE

OUTWARD EXPRESSIONS OF INWARD HIDDEN EMOTIONS

PERMANENT AND TEMPORARY ROLES

REVIEW – Fill in the Blanks

- Life is like a _____. We are all _____.
- There are usually four _____ roles we have in life: Relative, _____, Peer, and Other.
- Masks are a form of _____-_____.

OUTWARD EXPRESSIONS OF INWARD HIDDEN EMOTIONS

1. Read the poem.

THE MASK I WEAR

My surface may be smooth but my surface is my mask,
My ever-varying and ever-concealing mask.
Beneath lies no smugness, no complacency
Beneath dwells the real me in confusion, in fear, in aloneness.
   But I hide this.
    I don't want anybody to know it.
    I panic at the thought of my
       weaknesses
    and fear exposing them.
That's why I frantically create my masks
    to hide behind.
They're nonchalant, sophisticated facades
    to help me pretend,
To shield me from the glance that
    knows.
But such a glance is precisely my salvation,
   my only salvation,
    and I know it.

That is, if it's followed by acceptance,
   and if it's followed by love.
It's the only thing that can liberate me from myself
   from my own self-built prison walls

–Author Unknown

2. Underscore a line in the poem above that interests you. What do you think the author is saying in the line of text that you chose?

_____

_____

3. Can you identify with the author?   YES or **NO**

Wearing masks occasionally in our lives is part of human nature. It is common to switch masks depending on the occasion, setting, or audience.

4. Think of a party or an event you have attended recently. Now imagine you are telling your close friends about it. What things would you share? Write at least three things you would share with your close friends on a separate sheet of paper. No one will look at them; be honest.

5. Now, if you were telling your parents about this event, what information would you give them? Write at least three things you would share with your parents on the separate sheet of paper about the event.

6. How does the information that you gave to your parents differ from the information you gave your friends?

_____

_____

7. Think about a third group of people, for example your grandparents or your eight-year-old brother or nephew. What information would you share with them? Write at least three things you would share with your grandparents or your little brother or nephew on the separate sheet of paper.

8. How does this information given to close friends differ from the information you gave your parents, your grandparents, brother or nephew?

_____

_____

9. Did you respond differently to your friends than you did with your grandparents, brother or nephew, or parents?

YES or NO

10. In the scenario, you were playing different sub-roles of friend, son/daughter, grandchild, brother or uncle. Why might you have responded differently to the different groups of people?

_____

_____

11. How might you have responded if you would have shared the party information in the sub-roles of **child** and **friend**. For example, how would your story have changed if you were presenting the information to your **parents** and your **friends** at the same time?

_____

_____

PERMANENT AND TEMPORARY ROLES

We all have many roles to play in life. Often we play **two** or **more** roles at the same time. We may stop playing one or more roles to start the next one. Sometimes we get to choose roles of interest to us (for example, a friend); at other times, we have no choice in our role selection (for example, family).

In the last lesson you learned about role mapping and the four **power** roles: Family, Friend, Peer, and Other. You also identified the sub-roles you play in life. Sub-roles are classified as **permanent** or **temporary**.

If you are a daughter, you will always be a daughter, even if you or your parent dies. Likewise, when you become a parent, you will always be a parent, even when your child grows up or one of you deceases. However, you will most likely be a classmate temporarily, just until you finish school.

Additionally, you may be close friends with someone temporarily until you reach a certain age. With time your friends may change. It is common to change your close friends when you transition from high school to college or start working. Likewise, a close friend that you had in elementary school may be your close friend forever, a permanent sub-role.

12. Think about the roles that YOU play in life. Focus one specific role that you currently play. Then project yourself as being a 40-year-old person. Will YOU have the same role when you are older as you do now? If you believe you will have the same role when you are older, then it is a **permanent** role. If you cannot imagine yourself when you are older in the same role as you are now, then mark it as a **temporary** role.

13. Copy the sub-roles that you wrote in the circles in Lesson Two into the chart below. Then give each sub-role a Permanent or Temporary designation as you believe it to be for your life. Follow the examples given. Ignore the Emotion Column for now. Two examples are shown.

No.	Sub-Role	Permanent or Temporary	Emotion
A	Daughter	Permanent	Anger
B	Classmate	Temporary	Happiness
1			
2			
3			
4			
5			
6			
7			
8			
9			
10			
11			
12			
13			
14			

14. Next, refer to the Emotion Table below, and in the Emotion column above, write the emotion you mostly feel for each sub-role that you listed. The example shows that the reader plays a daughter role. The role is permanent, and the reader feels mostly anger in the daughter role. Follow this example for all your entries.

Emotion Table

Love	Fear	Happiness	Sadness	Anger	Surprise
😊	😮	😃	🙁	😠	😄
Relief	Gratitude	Satisfaction	Peacefulness	Adoration	Anxiety
😛	😌	🙂	😐	😊	😟

15. What emotion(s) did you list in the Emotion Column that you mostly felt?

_____

16. Using colored pencils or crayons, **draw a custom emoticon in the space below of the emotion that you most frequently wrote in the chart above.** For example, if you wrote the emotion "Fear" the most, then create a custom fear emoticon showing how fear feels to you.

LESSON FOUR

HUMAN NEEDS

THE PROTECTION MASK

PROCESSING OUR ENVIRONMENT

REVIEW – Fill in the Blanks

Confused Frustrated Silly

Normal Scared Grumpy

Mad Shocked Angry

Sad Happy Flirty

- Masks are a form of _____-_____.
- Often we play _____ or _____ roles at the same time.
- Sub-roles are classified as _____ or _____.

THE MASK I WEAR

I dislike hiding, honestly

I dislike the superficial game I'm playing,

   the superficial phony game.

I'd really like to be genuine and me.

But I need your help, your hand to hold

Even though my masks would tell you otherwise

That glance from you is the only thing that assures me

   of what I can't assure myself,

      that I'm really worth something. *—Author Unknown*

1. Circle one line from the poem above, and describe a time when your life compared to the poet's.

_____

HUMAN NEEDS

We all have human needs that must be met in order to thrive and survive in life. At some time in our lives our world may have been shaken and our needs not met. The power people (Family, Friends, Peers, and Others) in our lives may have let us down. Maybe our basic needs, such as food, were not met or were taken away. Some people do not get enough to eat on a regular basis.

Basic Needs		
Air	Water	Food

Society may have failed us. We may have felt unsafe or had our security threatened.

Safety and Security			
Home	Body	Money	Clothing

We may feel like we do not belong to any group or that no one loves us. We may feel like we have no one to talk to.

Sense of Belonging		
Someone to love us		Someone to talk to

Our self-esteem or confidence may have been crushed.

Self-Esteem		
Self-Respect		Confidence

Our opportunity for a good education could be hindered, or our dreams may be shattered.

Self-Actualization		
Education		Dreams

THE PROTECTION MASK

In many situations, we may be afraid of making a bad situation worse. We may think if the other person knew who we REALLY are behind the mask, they would think less of us. It can be times such as these when we wear the Protection Mask.

The Protection Mask is a defense mask that says, "I'm Afraid" of harm, judgment, rejection, or pain.

The Protection Mask is worn to self-protect against potential threats.

A threat is a statement, expression, possibility, person, or thing likely to cause fear, damage, or danger. We may wear the Protection Mask because we feel the other person or situation is a threat to us personally or to something we need in life.

When we are wearing the Protection Mask, we are hiding an inward emotion, but we may respond with a much different outward expression. These outward expressions may include: laughter, apologies, remorse, avoidance, self-justification, arguing, anger, approval, or false agreement.

2. In the five tables above, place an "X" in the boxes with the symbols to indicate needs that you have felt at some time in your life were threatened or taken away.

CONSIDER THE FOLLOWING:

Zach Larson invited Jacob to come over to his house for breakfast. Jacob rode his bike to the Larson's house, soaking in the morning sun as he coasted. The classmates resided on the same street. Parking his bike in the rear of the house, he entered, as he usually did, through the outside basement door. Stepping inside Jacob heard Mr. Larson shouting from above in the house. "You could have been in an accident! You are grounded for a month!" Mr. Larson's voice was loud and stern. A small stream of light trickled through to the basement from the small opening beside the door at the top of the stairs. Jacob stood quietly. Hidden by the shadows, he peered up the staircase. He watched a disturbing scene unfolding. Jacob saw Mr. Larson lunge forward. Something made of glass fell to the floor, shattering with a crash. Jacob heard his friend yell, "You don't listen to me like Mom did! I am a careful driver!" Zach ran into his room and slammed the door. Jacob inhaled a whiff of burnt toast as he nervously shifted his feet, and chewed his gum slowly. Suddenly Mr. Larson turned toward Jacob's direction. His icy stare only lasted a few seconds, but it seemed like a long time. Jacob shivered as his empty stomach growled. Jacob tightly gripped the cold stair railing. Without saying a word, Jacob turned and slipped out of the basement, headed for home.

ANALYZING ZACH AND MR. LARSON

3. Read the paragraph above. In the appropriate cells in the table below, write the outward expressions, words, actions, and the inward emotion you believe were displayed by Mr. Larson and Zach.

MR. LARSON		INWARD EMOTION	ZACH		INWARD EMOTION
Outward Expression:			Outward Expression:		
Words:			Words:		
Actions:			Actions:		

4. In the five tables at the beginning of this lesson, place a "Z" in the white space by the symbols which represent the needs in Zach's life that appear to have been threatened based on the event you read about.

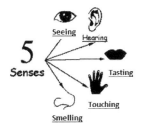

PROCESSING OUR ENVIRONMENT

The processing of our environment begins with **data intake** by any of our **five** senses. The processing of our environment ends with the production of thoughts which may result in **words** and **actions**. This is a **response** to what we have experienced.

Jacob witnessed a troubling scene at Zach's house. The information collected by his five **senses** will create a **memory** of the experience and produce thoughts. As a result, Jacob may produce **words** or **actions**.

5. What **information** did Jacob take in through his five **senses** during the scene with Zach and Mr. Larson?

What did Jacob HEAR?	
What did Jacob SEE?	
What did Jacob SMELL?	
What did Jacob TASTE?	
What did Jacob FEEL?	

6. In the appropriate cells in the table below, write the outward expressions, words, actions, and the inward emotion you believe were displayed by Jacob.

JACOB	INWARD EMOTION
Outward Expression:	
Words:	
Actions:	

Fight or Flight Syndrome is an involuntary response to a stressful situation in which the hormone **adrenaline** is secreted into the blood in readiness for physical action, such as **fighting** or **running away**.

Refer to the story on the previous page. Circle the answer.

7. Did Mr. Larson FIGHT or RUN AWAY?
8. Did Zach FIGHT or RUN AWAY?
9. Did Jacob FIGHT or RUN AWAY?

LESSON FIVE

INTERPRETATION OF DATA

NEW FACTS, NEW PERCEPTIONS

REVIEW – Fill in the Blanks

- We all have human needs that must be met in order to _____ and _____ in life.
- The **Protection Mask** is a defense mask that says, "_____ _____."
- A _____ is a statement, expression, possibility, person, or thing likely to cause fear, damage, or danger.
- _____ or _____ Syndrome is an involuntary response to a _____ situation.

INTERPRETATION OF DATA

The interpretation of data collected from our environment begins with its intake through any of the five senses. In Lesson 4, you read a short story about Jacob. You mapped Jacob's five senses, outward expression, words, actions, and inward emotions. Let's interpret other elements of Jacob's experience at Zach's house.

1. Pretend that you are Jacob. Without looking at the story, what is your memory of the short story about Jacob's visit at Zach's house? Rewrite a summary of the story from **memory** in your own words as Jacob. Use another sheet of paper if necessary.

_____

_____

_____

_____

2. Since Jacob's story was "just a story", and you were not personally impacted. Therefore, you may not remember key facts. Go back and reread the story in Lesson 4. List below any facts that you forgot to write about above from your **memory**.

_____

_____

3. Write about a **memory** from your personal life that causes you to feel a strong emotion. Who was involved in your memory? A family member, friend, peer, or another person? When you think about that person(s), what **emotion** do you feel the strongest? Use another sheet of paper if necessary.

_____

_____

When you think from memory, you may remember some facts about the situation. You most likely remember how the situation made you feel. You remember how you perceived the situation. Perception is what we acquire when we combine facts with our feelings. Perception is how we understand or interrupt a situation. It is a mental impression. The memory of facts, feelings, and your perception of the data collected by your five senses have enabled you to develop beliefs about the situation.

Just because we have a memory about a situation and have formed a belief from the facts, feelings or perceptions, we may not know the entire TRUTH about the situation. Therefore, our beliefs may not be accurate.

It is said that our perception is our realty. Our perception may be different from someone else's perception. This means two people who witness the same event and may have a different story about the event.

4. Look at the graphic below, who is the most accurate in perceiving the correct number of logs; the person on the left or the person on the right? Explain your answer in the space below.

_____

_____

5. Perception is formed by the information that our five senses collect along with the emotions that we feel. Think about our story, and pretend that you are Jacob. Consider the information Jacob might have collected through his five senses. What emotions might Jacob have felt while witnessing the event. What is your perception of Mr. Larson? How do you see him as a person, a father, and neighbor? What kind of person is he?

_____

_____

6. A **belief** is being **sure** that something is true. It takes into account not only the information we perceived through our five senses but the emotions we felt at the time. It also includes any memories or knowledge we have of similar experiences from the past. What do you believe about Mr. Larson? Complete the following: I believe Mr. Larson:

_____

_____

A **fact** is a piece of **true** information. We can learn the whole truth when we have ALL of the facts. Considering other points of view may cause us to change our perception.

The truth about Mr. Larson's actions are hidden behind the outward mask of anger. Until we

know what Mr. Larson is angry about, we can't understand his actions.

Remember, the Protection Mask is a defense mask that says, "I'm Afraid" of harm, judgment, rejection, or pain.

Types of outward expressions of fear may include arguing and/or anger.

7. Anger and arguing were the outward expressions of Mr. Larson and Zack. What might Mr. Larson be afraid of?

_____

_____

8. What might Zach be afraid of?

_____

_____

NEW FACTS, NEW PERCEPTIONS

A week had passed since Jacob witnessed the troubling event at his friend Zach's house. It was a school day, but Jacob felt ill and didn't attend that day. The doorbell rang at Jacob's house. Jacob stood in the background as his mother answered. Yikes! There stood Mr. Larson with fresh flowers for his Mom. Jacob's mom, Ms. Barren, returned a smile to Mr. Larson. Mr. Larson's eyes focused, and he spotted Jacob in the shadows. "Uh, h-h-hello Jacob," Mr. Larson stammered as his face reddened. "I'm sorry Ms. Barren, if I've barged in. I truly am. I didn't mean to intrude." He babbled, "I can come back at another time." Jacob turned and retreated to his bedroom. Ms. Barren yelled after him, "Jacob, come back here, and greet our nice neighbor Mr. Larson."

9. Refer to the mask graphic on the previous page. What outward expression(s) did Mr. Larson exhibit when he saw Jacob?

_____

10. Refer again to the mask graphic. What outward expression(s) did Jacob exhibit when he saw Mr. Larson?

_____

When we don't address our feelings it is a sign of avoidance.

11. Why might Mr. Larson be afraid of Jacob?

_____

12. Why might Jacob be afraid of Mr. Larson?

_____

13. Is Jacob fighting or running away from Mr. Larson?   FIGHT   RUNNING AWAY

14. Do you think Mr. Larson will fight or run away from Jacob?   FIGHT   RUN AWAY

15. Do you think that Mr. Larson being nice to Jacob's mom has changed Jacob's beliefs about him? YES or NO

What if you found out the following additional facts about Mr. Larson and Zach?

- Zach's mother passed away in a car accident. She was hit by a drunk driver.
- The day that Jacob heard the altercation, Mr. Larson, Zach's father, had just learned that Zach had driven his father's car without his permission.

16. Knowing these new facts, complete the following: I believe Mr. Larson:

_____

_____

17. Has your perception (your mental impression) of Mr. Larson changed considering the

   addition of the new facts?   YES or NO

18. Have your beliefs (what you are sure is true) changed about Mr. Larson? YES or NO

19. Draw the characters (Mr. Larson, Zach, Jacob, and Ms. Barren) of our story as stick people below. On the faces of the stick persons, draw the emotion that they most likely feel as prominent in their heart. Identify the inward emotion.

LESSON SIX

UNMASKING EMOTIONS

THE EFFECTS OF GRIEF

REVIEW – Fill in the Blanks

- _____ is an interpretation of a situation based upon the information that our five senses collect along with the _____ that we feel.
- A _____ is being sure something is true.
- We can learn the whole _____ when we have ALL of the _____.

UNMASKING EMOTIONS

In order to understand what is behind the masks of the characters in our story, we must work to unmask the hidden emotions. This is usually not a quick or easy task. We will have to break down the events in hopes of gaining insight to the emotions.

1. In a previous lesson, you learned that the day of the quarrel at Zach's house, Mr. Larson, Zach's father, had just learned that Zach had driven his father's car without his permission.

2. Reread the short story.

Zach Larson invited Jacob to come over to his house for breakfast. Jacob rode his bike to the Larson's house, soaking in the morning sun as he coasted. The classmates resided on the same street. Parking his bike in the rear of the house, he entered, as he usually did, through the outside basement door. Stepping inside Jacob heard Mr. Larson shouting from above in the house. "You could have been in an accident! You are grounded for a month!" Mr. Larson's voice was loud and stern. A small stream of light trickled through to the basement from the small opening beside the door at the top of the stairs. Jacob stood quietly. Hidden by the shadows, he peered up the staircase. He watched a disturbing scene unfolding. Jacob saw Mr. Larson lunge forward. Something made of glass fell to the floor, shattering with a crash. Jacob heard his friend yell, "You don't listen to me like Mom did! I am a careful driver!" Zach ran into his room and slammed the door. Jacob inhaled a whiff of burnt toast as he nervously shifted his feet, and chewed his gum slowly. Suddenly Mr. Larson turned toward Jacob's direction. His icy stare only lasted a few seconds, but it seemed like a long time. Jacob shivered as his empty stomach growled. Jacob tightly gripped the cold stair railing. Without saying a word, Jacob turned and slipped out of the basement, headed for home.

As our short story demonstrates, it is often difficult to know the whole truth of a situation by only observing some of the facts. The person wearing the mask knows the inside information as they perceive it. The painful information that we perceive is felt as a deep emotion in our heart. Our outward response due to the emotion we feel in our heart may result in negative consequences to ourselves or others. An outward expression is often a reaction to what we feel inwardly. When we feel pain in our hearts we may respond with an angry outburst in our words and/or actions. Our angry reaction can hurt others which in turn may give us a guilty feeling in addition to the original pain, compounding our hurt.

The process of **unmasking** emotions can be complicated. It is often difficult to resolve the matter until we know the original cause of pain. As we seek to understand and be understood we can make progress to help ourselves or others through a painful situation.

THE EFFECTS OF GRIEF

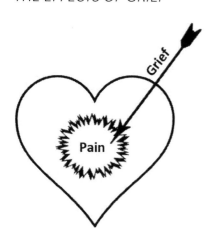

Mr. Larson and Zach are grieving. Grief is the process of deep sorrow we feel over the loss of **someone** or **something** very dear to us. Grief feels like a dart to the heart. Grief causes us to feel pain in our heart. Mr. Larson and Zach suffered a severe loss when Mrs. Larson died in a car accident. They are both sad and angry about their loss. There is no right or wrong way to grieve, and there is no specified length of time for grieving. We are all different. The more **significant** the loss, the **longer** it may take to go through the grieving process. It is important to know that there are healthy ways to cope with the pain. In time, it is usually possible to move on with our lives and be able to live a productive life. Healing is encouraged when we give honor to our loved one(s) and/or a cause to help others.

There are five foundational emotions of the grieving process. Even though there is a "typical" order of emotions, an individual can experience any one of them at any time. The five are:

Surprise/Shock	Guilt	Sadness	Anger	Acceptance
😃	😖	🙁	😠	😐
Felt when an unexpected piece of information is received	A bad feeling caused by knowing or thinking that you have done something bad or wrong	Feeling grief or unhappiness	Strong feeling of being upset, threatening	To recognize as true

Complete the following by writing in an emotion from the chart above or by explaining the emotion as requested.

3. Mr. Larson was _____ when he found out that Mrs. Larson died in a car accident.

4. Mr. Larson felt _____ because he thought the accident might not have happened, if he had driven Mrs. Larson to work on the day of the accident.

5. Many evenings after work, Mr. Larson felt _____, when he went home to an empty house. His son, Zach, spent lots of time at his friend Jacob's house.

6. Mr. Larson punched his pillow. Life wasn't fair. He felt _____ that his wife died due to the recklessness of a drunk driver.

7. Finally, Mr. Larson must _____ the undesirable truth, that life must go on.

8. Review your answers above for questions #2 - #6. Is Mr. Larson **guilty** of anything in regards to the accident?   YES   or **NO**

9. Which of the five grief emotions will help Mr. Larson combat the feeling of guilt? Explain your answer.

_____

_____

A **trigger** is when something happens that reminds us of an occasion or loss. It is data taken in through our **five senses** that triggers **memories** and **thoughts** that remind us of another event and the **feelings** associated with the other event.

When Mr. Larson sees Mrs. Larson's photo, thoughts and memories are triggered, and he feels the pain of his loss. The graphic shows how a trigger works.

10. What event happened in our story that might have triggered Mr. Larson to react to Zach in anger?

_____

_____

_____

A **trigger** can cause us to bounce from one emotion to the other. It can come when we least expect it.

11. One evening Mr. Larson was watching the news, and he experienced a trigger of the emotion of **sadness**. What might Mr. Larson have heard on the evening news that would be a trigger for sadness?

_____

_____

12. What other emotion(s) might escalate when Mr. Larson is triggered and feels the emotion of sadness?

_____

13. Describe a time that your memory and emotions were triggered. Explain the following: What was the **trigger**, which of your **five senses** (something you saw, heard, tasted, felt, or smelled) were used to activate the trigger, what was your **memory**, and what **emotions** did you feel? Use other paper if necessary.

_____

_____

14. Reread Scene 2 of our story.

THE STORY – SCENE 2

A week had passed since Jacob witnessed the troubling event at his friend Zach's house. It was a school day, but Jacob felt ill and didn't attend that day. The doorbell rang at Jacob's house. Jacob stood in the background as his mother answered. Yikes! There stood Mr. Larson with fresh flowers for his Mom. Jacob's mom, Ms. Barren, returned a smile to Mr. Larson. Mr. Larson's eyes focused, and he spotted Jacob in the shadows. "Uh, h-h-hello Jacob," Mr. Larson stammered as his face reddened. "I'm sorry Ms. Barren, if I've barged in. I truly am. I didn't mean to intrude." He babbled, "I can come back at another time." Jacob turned and retreated to his bedroom. Ms. Barren yelled after him, "Jacob, come back here, and greet our nice neighbor Mr. Larson."

15. Name an emotion in the grieving process exhibited by Mr. Larson in Scene 2. Also state how Mr. Larson is specifically responding to the emotions.

_____

_____

LESSON SEVEN

INHERITED AND LEARNED TRAITS

IMPACTS OF LIFE

REVIEW – Fill in the Blanks

- The process of _____ our emotions can be complicated.
- The more _____ the loss, the _____ it may take to go through the grieving process.
- A _____ is when something happens that reminds us of an occasion or loss.

INHERITED AND LEARNED TRAITS

We all have inherited and learned traits or behaviors. These traits can have negative or positive outcomes in our life. The combination of inherited and learned traits gives us our roots and our personality. The inherited traits are considered genetic, and the learned traits are considered experience.

Inherited Traits

Inherited traits are passed to a child from the biological parent. Inherited traits are genetic. There is a degree of probability that a child will have the genes of the parents. Examples of traits that may be passed on with a degree of probability are: IQ, depression, anxiety, and weight gain.

Just because you inherit a trait does not mean that it will manifest itself in your life. The trait may remain dormant for your entire life, or it may be triggered by an impact in life.

For example, Mrs. Larson, Zach's mother, carried the depression trait. She passed that trait on to Zach, her son. The trait could have remained dormant for Zach's entire life, but when he suffered the tragic loss of his mother, the trait was triggered and became active.

As you have learned, sadness is an emotion experienced in the cycle of grief. Depression is when we feel extreme sadness or hopelessness. Zach had the tendency to feel extreme sadness. In addition to the sadness from his loss, his mother's trait of depression will most likely be triggered. Zach should be aware that there is a good probability that the extreme sadness he feels may affect his mental health.

Learned Traits

Learned traits are our life experiences. There are learned traits that appear to be inherited. These traits include: IQ, depression, anxiety, and weight gain. If the traits are learned and not inherited, with effort they may be altered. Learned traits are acquired through experience.

For example, you may have grown up in a family where you were not taught how to eat healthy foods. As a result, you gained weight due to learned behavior rather than inherited genes. However, once you learn about healthy eating you can unlearn the unhealthy eating behavior and lose weight.

Mr. Larson inherited a trait of anxiety. He is frequently worried and wonders "What if..." Zach does not seem to worry about life to the extent his father does. There is a good probability that the more Zach observes his father's worried behavior, the greater Zach's chances are of experiencing anxiety. This learned behavior can affect his mental health. If this is the case, Zach will have to learn a way to overcome what he has learned in order to improve his mental health.

1. Stick out your tongue. Try to roll the edges toward the middle of your tongue. Can you do it? Is this an inherited or learned trait?

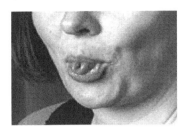

2. Humans inherit some traits from their parents and others they learn. In the chart below, place an 'X' in the correct column to identify each trait as either inherited or learned.

Unique Traits

In addition to our inherited and learned traits, we each have unique traits that are exclusive to us. For example, your mom and dad cannot sing, but you are a good singer. Singing is a unique trait you have. It gives you part of your individuality. Your unique trait may be a result of a combination of traits from your parents or grandparents.

Trait	Inherited	Learned
Green Eyes		
Freckles		
Juggling		
Rolling your Tongue		
Riding a Bicycle		

You can also develop your own traits through intellect, hobbies, and interests. For example, you may learn to be a rock climber through training. This is a trait that you could teach to your children. It would be a learned behavior for them.

3. Fill in the answers below.

A trait that I have inherited is:	
A trait that I have learned is:	
Unique Traits that I have that no one else in my family have are:	

IMPACTS OF LIFE

The traits that we exhibit, both inherited (genetic) and learned (experience), plays a role when our lives are impacted by events. We are **impacted** when something happens that has a strong negative effect. We all have impacts in our life. Impacts can have a temporary or permanent effect on our lives. Impacts can slow us down in obtaining our goals in life. Impacts come in five types. You have already learned about two of these (genetic and experience). Negative impacts are defined below and identified by a symbol.

Impact Chart

Impacts	Inherited Traits
A. Genetic	Inherited traits or behaviors are those which are **genetically** passed or capable of being passed from parent to offspring. **Inherited** impacts are involuntary. Examples of **inherited** traits are eye color, height, skin color, and diseases.
B. Experience	Learned Traits Learned traits or behaviors are caused by our experiences or observations. Examples of **learned** traits are your sense of humor, manners, food preferences, and religious customs. **Learned** impacts are at first **involuntary**. With effort we have a **voluntary** option to overcome and change learned traits.
C. Physical	A **physical** impact is an injury to our bodies which affects the functionality of our brain or body. A birth defect, accident, reaction to medication, physical mistreatment, or physical illness are examples. Physical impacts are **usually** involuntary.
D. Psychological	A **psychological** impact is an injury or trauma (such as threats, worry, overwhelmed, lack of security, or lack of self-esteem). Impacts affect the mind or feelings. Psychological impacts are **involuntary**.
E. Environmental	An environmental impact is a loss of things in our environment. Environmental impacts include: death, divorce, home, safety, employment, and basic needs [water, food, and shelter]. Environmental impacts may be voluntary or involuntary. An environmental impact can trigger a psychological impact.

When we are faced with one of the five types of impacts our lives will be affected. The responses and the results of the impacts will shape who we are and aid in the development of our personality.

The diagram below shows the traits that Zach inherited and learned. Inherited traits are present at birth, but some may not be realized until later in life. Zach's inherited and learned traits became reality when an environmental impact (losing his mother) occurred.

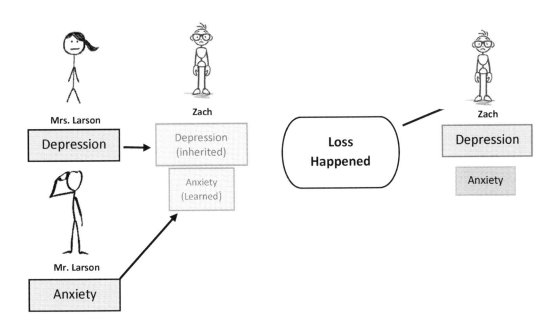

4. Remembering the story of Zach, what traits might Zach **learn** from his father based on his father's reaction to him driving without permission?

_____

_____

Refer to the impact definitions and the symbols in the Impact chart above for the exercise below.

5. Knowing the information you have learned about Mr. Larson and Zach, write a brief description of the impacts experienced by Mr. Larson and Zach as indicated by the symbols below. Add any extra impacts in the blank rows, by drawing the symbol and writing a description.

Description of Mr. Larson's Impacts		Description of Zach's Impacts	
△	Genetics	△	Genetics
▭	Environmental	✦	Experience
⬤	Psychological	▭	Environmental
⬤	Psychological	⬤	Psychological
		⬤	Psychological

6. Draw the corresponding symbols below indicating which of the five **impacts** you have experienced in your life.

Remember, Zach's **genetically** inherited traits were triggered when an **environmental** impact occurred in his life.

7. Refer to a symbol that you drew above. Think about the traits that you have **inherited** or **learned** from your parents or next of kin, (such as aunts, uncles, adoptive parents, older siblings). Describe how your **inherited** or **learned** traits which have affected your response to an event in your life. Describe an event in your life when you responded like your parents would have

_____

_____

_____

LESSON EIGHT

IMPACTS AND MENTAL HEALTH

WHAT IS MENTAL ILLNESS

MENTAL HEALTH FACTORS

REVIEW – Fill in the Blanks

- Inherited traits or learned behaviors are _____ passed from parent to offspring.
- Learned traits or behaviors are caused by _____ or _____.
- A _____ impact is an injury or change to our physical bodies affecting the physical functionality of our brain or body.
- A _____ impact is an injury or trauma affecting the mind or feelings.
- An _____ impact is a loss of physical things around us.

IMPACTS AND MENTAL HEALTH

You have learned the five main types of impacts are: Genetic, Experience, Physical, Psychological, and Environmental. At some point in life, we all experience impacts. Our response to impacts will project our path to

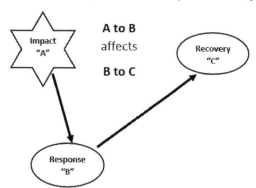

recovery from the impact. The severity of the impact affects our response. The longer it takes for us to respond, the longer it will take to recover. The longer it takes to recover, the more affect there will be on our mental health. It is important that we respond in a way that will combat any negative outcomes of the impact. For example, if we need professional help, it is important that we get help as early as possible for a faster recovery. In this lesson we will learn about mental health and the difference between mental health and mental illness. First we will contrast mental health with physical health.

Physical Health

If we do not care for our bodies, and we are exposed to germs or disease, we may become physically ill. In order to treat our physical health, we first have to recognize the symptoms such as sneezing, sore throat, or coughing. Once we analyze our symptoms, it becomes easier to identify the illness.

It is important to determine the source of the illness. Is the source involuntary? For example, is it something that we were born with, or is it something we have acquired as a result of our environment? Can we voluntarily change the environment and improve our situation? For example, we should be careful not to be around others with the flu. But if we live with a smoker, we may not be able to change our environment. Both situations may leave us with physical symptoms, and when our physical health is affected, our mental health is at risk.

Treatment of the illness may include:

- home remedy (e.g., rest, eat healthy, drink hot teas),
- taking over the counter medications,
- going to the doctor, or
- taking instructed prescription medications.

1. Describe a time in your life when you were physically sick. What were your symptoms?

_____

_____

2. What was your illness? How was the illness acquired?

_____

_____

3. Did you change anything in your environment (where you were or who you were around) to help alleviate the illness? What did you do to treat the illness?

_____

_____

Mental Health

We all have physical health, and we all have mental health. As we can get a "cold" physically or "the flu," we can become **depressed** or have **anxiety**. We will learn more about depression and anxiety in this study.

The World Health Organization defines **Mental Health** using a **Four-Way Test**. The four ways define **a state of well-being** in which the individual:

- realizes his or her own **potential**.
- can **cope** with the normal stresses of life.
- can **work** productively.
- is able to make a **contribution** to the community.

Refer to the bullets of the **Four-Way Test**, and complete the following by filling in the blanks.

4. In my future career, I have the potential to be_____.

5. X = something that is stressful and happens frequently in my life. When X happens, I do the

   following to cope with X:_____

_____

6. One thing that I can do well in life and see results is _____

_____.

7. One way I can give back to my community is _____.

We **recognized** the emotional symptoms of **fear** such as **arguing**, **anger**, and **grief** in Zach's story. We learned that the **source** of the fear was **environmental** and **involuntary** through the loss of a loved one. We learned that an environmental loss triggered a psychological impact. We also learned that Zach's pain was compounded through genetics by his inherited traits of depression and his learned traits of anxiety.

Often our physical symptoms may be a result of an emotional symptom. Emotional symptoms produce **physical** symptoms. When you get angry you may feel your face getting hot, your jaw tightening, or your fist clenching.

Just as there are procedures to treat a **physical illness**, there are procedures to treat **mental health**. The **steps** to care for both our physical and mental health are:

1) Recognize the symptoms.
2) Identify the type of illness.
3) Determine the source.
4) Change the contributing environment, (if possible).
5) Treat the illness.

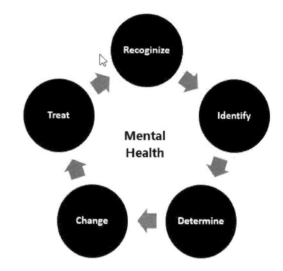

You have learned several techniques in this workbook on how to **care** for your mental health. So far, you have learned to:

1) Recognize the symptoms by identifying your emotions and human needs.
2) Determine the source by understanding the impacts of life.
3) Change the contributing environment, if possible by being aware of your environment through the five senses.

You will continue to learn **preventive** techniques to care for your mind throughout this workbook. You will also understand the importance of **identifying** and **treating** mental Illness.

You should know that unhealthy **mental health may not be your fault**. There are **preventive** and **long-term** treatments to help offset the effects of its negative **impacts** in your life.

WHAT IS MENTAL ILLNESS?

Mental Illness is a condition that affects a person's thinking, feeling, or mood. Such conditions may affect someone's ability to relate to others and function each day. Each person will have different experiences, even people with the same diagnosis. We all have experienced the symptoms of mental illness at some point in our life.

Mental illness symptoms may include:

- a marked personality change
- an inability to cope
- excessive anxiety
- prolonged depression or apathy
- marked changes in eating or sleeping patterns
- extreme emotional highs and lows, and
- excessive anger, hostility, or violent behavior.

We cross over from "a state of well-being" or "healthy" mental health to a "unhealthy" mental health or mental illness, when we can no longer control our symptoms.

Refer back to the Mental Health Four-Way Test above and answer the following.

8. We may experience mental illness when we do not realize our _____, cannot _____ with the normal stresses of life, cannot _____ productively, or are not able to make a _____ back to our community.

MENTAL HEALTH FACTORS

Some of the top factors that may trigger mental illness are:

- Low Self-Esteem
- Feeling Unloved
- Low Confidence
- Family Breakup (Divorce)
- Loss (includes Death or Illness)
- Physical Illness
- Being a Caregiver
- Being Bullied at School
- Substance Abuse
- Living in Poverty
- Being Abused

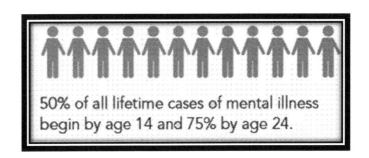

50% of all lifetime cases of mental illness begin by age 14 and 75% by age 24.

We know that how we respond and recover to the five major impacts (Genetic, Experience, Physical, Psychological, and Environmental) in life are keys to combating mental illness.

Positive responses to life impacts may include:
- keeping your body healthy
- connecting with people who care for you
- staying involved with activities that help you build confidence
- learning about topics that interest you
- knowing that you have a purpose in life
- giving back to your community
- doing something productive for yourself or others
- having gratitude
- seeking counseling
- forgives toward those who have hurt you (this doesn't mean you like or agree with them)

Negative responses to life impacts may include:
- eating junk food
- hanging with friends who will lead you down a path that leads to negative results
- participating in substance abuse
- isolating yourself from others
- bullying others
- spending too much time with technology instead of caring friends
- unforgiveness toward those who have hurt you
- being an overachiever
- becoming bitter

9. Describe a situation where one of the mental health factors listed above had a negative effect on you, a friend, or family member. Apply the Four-Way Test. Which of the four ways failed as a result of the situation? Describe what could have been done differently for a more positive result.

_____

_____

We all have mental health. Many of us may experience a mental illness or know a friend or family member who does.

Statics show that 50% of mental illness begins by age 14 and 75% by age 24. One in five children will experience a mental illness. By the time they are adults it becomes one in four.

10. What could you do for someone who is experiencing mental illness to bring hope to them?

_____

LESSON NINE

DEPRESSION AND ANXIETY

REVIEW – Fill in the Blanks

- Our _____ to life's impacts will project our path to _____ from the impact.
- When our _____ health is affected, our _____ health is at risk.
- The World Health Organization defines mental health as a state of _____ - _____.

DEPRESSION AND ANXIETY

Are you physically healthy? The healthier we are physically, the stronger we are emotionally. The heaviness or the load of life is what we feel when we are weighted down emotionally or physically. The unhealthier we are, the heavier the load. Our physical and mental health is affected by the severity and the frequency of life impacts - Genetic, Experience, Physical, Psychological, and Environmental.

Depression and anxiety are alerts that our mental health needs attention. Depression and anxiety are common symptoms of many mental illnesses. Depression has been called the "common cold" of mental health. As with all human traits, we may have genetically inherited a more likely chance of becoming depressed or anxious. However, you can learn ways to cope with these two alerts.

What exactly are depression and anxiety?

Depression is a state of feeling sad.

Anxiety is worry or fear about what might happen.

Typically, depression and anxiety are the results of life's negative impacts. These symptoms can be fleeting or long lasting, but they serve as a reminder we need to take care of ourselves.

We can think of the symptoms of sadness (depression) and/or fear (anxiety) as alerts.

Everyone is depressed at times. It is normal to feel depressed when something bad happens to us. But extreme depression is continued sadness even when everyone around us is happy.

When we frequently feel sad, hopeless, unimportant, or are unable to live a productive life, then our mental health is at risk.

Extreme Depression

1. Describe a time that you felt sad when everyone else around you appeared to be happy. How long were you in that state of mind?

_____

_____

Everyone is anxious or worried at times. It is normal to feel anxious when something stable changes in our life. However, **extreme anxiety** is feeling fear or apprehension when our surrounding is constant or unchanged.

If you consistently feel panic, fear, apprehension, or nervousness causing interference with routine tasks, then your mental health is at risk.

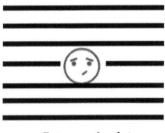

Extreme Anxiety

2. Describe a time when you felt anxious about something that might happen in the future, even though your situation was unchanged. Did what you were worried about really happen?

_____

_____

Emotion Meter

The Emotion Meter below shows how our feelings may go from being happy to being peaceful, to sad, to anxious, to depression or anxiety.

If our feelings get stuck in the anxiety or depression state, then <u>it is at that point we are dealing with mental illness symptoms.</u>

3. Reflecting back on Zach's story, complete the charts below. Describe an event that may have caused feelings of **depression** and **anxiety** for Mr. Larson and Zach. Place a check to show if you believe the causes will present a short-term or long-term challenge.

Mr. Larson			
What caused feelings of DEPRESSION?		Short Term	Long Term

Zach			
What caused feelings of DEPRESSION?		Short Term	Long Term

Mr. Larson			
What caused feelings of ANXIETY?		Short Term	Long Term

Zach			
What caused feelings of ANXIETY?		Short Term	Long Term

 Once our emotion meter hits the depression or anxiety state, we may experience the "off the chart' feelings of hopelessness or fear. This escalation is illustrated in our story where we learned that Zach inherited his mother's genes of **depression**, and he **learned anxiety** from his father. Zach may be on a path of emotional escalation to anger.

4. Consider Zach's inherited genetic trait of depression. Where might he fit on the Emotion Path below? Do you think his **depression** will escalate to **nostalgia**? Nostalgia is a feeling of longing for things the way they were. Might Zach long for the way things were when his mother was alive? Will the realization of never having another moment with his mother cause Zach to feel **hopelessness**? Once the feeling of hopelessness is realized, one may feel anger. Pretend you are Zach. _Draw a stick figure on the graphic below to show where you would be on the depression path to anger if you were Zach._

Emotion Path

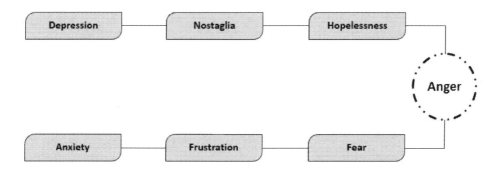

5. Now, consider Zach's learned trait of anxiety. Where might he fit on the Emotion Path above? Do you think Zach will feel **anxiety** when he worries about what he will do without a mother? Might his worries turn into **frustration**? Will Zach become frustrated because he realizes he cannot fix the situation? Do you think Zach will feel **fear** of what might happen if he loses his father? Will he become **angry** because something bad has happened to him that is beyond his control? Pretend you are Zach. *Draw a stick figure on the graphic below to show where you would be on the anxiety path to anger if you were Zach.*

6. Will Zach's **fear** or **hopelessness** escalate to **anger**? Who will he be angry at? Will his anger be directed toward the drunk driver who was responsible for his mother's death? Will he be **angry** toward a supreme being for allowing the accident to happen? Will he feel **anger** at himself for something he should have done to have prevented the accident? *Describe below what you think may cause Zach to feel anger. Will he be angry at himself or others (the drunk driver, a supreme being, etc.) or both?*

_____

_____

7. **Anger** is a strong feeling of displeasure or revenge. Tell about a time when you were angry. Did the anger start with something that depressed you or something that worried you? Did you want revenge? What made you angry?

_____

_____

LESSON TEN

THE ANGER CYCLE

DARTS TO THE HEART

REVIEW – Fill in the Blanks

- Our _____ and _____ health is affected by the severity and the frequency of life impacts - Genetic, Experience, Physical, Psychological, and Environmental.
- _____ is a state of feeling sad.
- _____ is worry or fear about what might happen.
- Extreme _____ is continued sadness even when everyone around is happy.
- Extreme _____ is feeling fear or apprehension when our surrounding is constant or unchanged.

THE ANGER CYCLE

We learned that depression can lead to feelings of hopelessness, and anxiety can lead to feelings of fear. These two major feelings often precede the feeling of anger. Anxiety and depression can feed on each other and form a vicious cycle. The cycle is intensified when we reach the stage of anger. We feel depressed or worried and then we feel anger. The feeling of anger makes us feel depressed and worried even more so.

We have learned that types of fear include: fear of harm, judgment, rejection, pain, or other things. In parallel to fear, we can also feel hopelessness. At the root of hopelessness and fear is anxiety and depression. These two mental health symptoms, depression and anxiety, may escalate to anger.

Zach's emotions emerged from pain he felt from the loss of someone in his personal environment in the power role of family. Grief can bring feelings of guilt which can lead to feelings of anxiety and sadness and then result in depression and anger.

Zach was experiencing grief. In addition to the depression and anxiety Zach felt from his loss, he had inherited the depression trait and learned the trait of anxiety from his parents. The genetic and experience impacts presented the potential to weaken his mental health. He was hurting in his sub-role as son, and his mental health was very much at risk.

Zach felt fear from the pain of his loss. We are going to examine other fear scenarios. We will see how harm, judgment, and rejection relates to depression, anxiety, and anger.

Researchers believe that both our heart and our brain are emotion centers. Indicators show that our **heart** functions as our **emotional brain**, and our brain functions as our **rational brain**. It is believed that the emotional brain (**heart**) is the strongest of the two emotion centers. The **heart** brain may function up to 80%, leaving our **rational** brain to function at 20%. <u>This means that most of the time our **heart** overpowers our brain.</u> Our brain provides thoughts that rationalize how our heart feels.

<u>Harm</u>

Andrew instinctively jumped as his stepfather threw open the door and stood menacingly in the threshold. Andrew's shoulders and chest tightened as he gripped a glass of water. He felt the

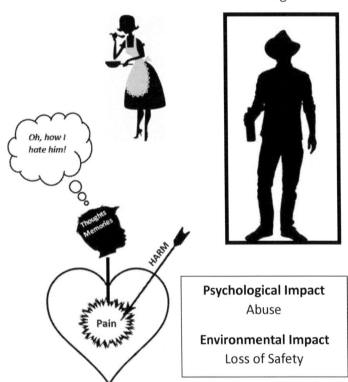

cold moisture on the glass mix with the hot sweat of his palms. The odor of cheap alcohol filled the air as his stepfather blurted obscenities toward his mother. "*Oh, how I hate him!*" thought Andrew. "*If he hits my mother again, I'm gonna punch his face!*"

Andrew's mind screamed, but he held his lips in tight silence. He knew what would happen, if he intervened. The pain in Andrew's right calf served as a reminder of what could happen, if he stood up for himself or his mother. Andrew's mother nervously stirred the beans and rice she was fixing for dinner. Andrew saw her hands shaking. As his stepfather moved in his direction, the cell phone in the man's pocket suddenly rang. "Yeah," his stepfather barked into the phone, "OK, I'll be right over." His cold eyes lingered as he smirked in Andrew's direction. Then he turned and walked out the door. Andrew let out a long sigh of relief relaxing his shoulders. His mother collapsed into a chair. Suddenly, Andrew remembered that he had his crumbled report card in his book bag. "*Another F,*" he thought. "*I can't tell my mother I failed, and that I got in trouble again for fighting. She's been through too much.*" Andrew felt he had not only failed his class, but he had let his mother down. Andrew closed his eyes and hung his head in despair.

1. Andrew's pain is coming from his fear of **harm**. Circle the emotions on the Emotion Path below which Andrew may be feeling. Describe in the blank space which emotion you believe he is feeling the strongest and why.

<u>Emotion Path</u>

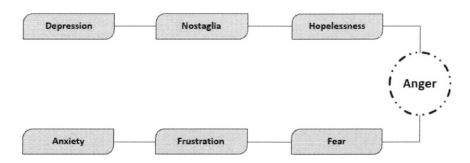

2. How do Andrew's thoughts (*"Oh, how I hate him*!" and *"If he hits my mother again, I'm gonna punch his face!"*) rationalize the **pain** of **harm** that his heart is feeling?

_____

3. Will it be easy for Andrew to change his thoughts? Is it to Andrew's benefit to change his view? Does Andrew hate his stepfather or the harmful situation he fosters? What might Andrew do to get help for himself and his mother?

_____

When fear is compounded with depression or anxiety, our outward actions may indicate something totally different such as: **laughter, apologies, remorse, avoidance, self-justification, arguing,** or **anger.**

4. In school Andrew is the class clown. He frequently makes jokes and wisecracks when the teacher asks him a question or when other students speak to him. Why might Andrew act this way? What mask is he wearing? Why does Andrew need his classmates' response of laughter?

_____

<u>Judgement</u>

Madison's teacher, Mrs. Smith, was out on long-term leave. Ms. Vone was substituting. Madison quietly entered the noisy classroom and slipped uneasily into her desk. She always dreaded having a new teacher, because a new teacher might call upon her to read. Madison was born with a learning disability called dyslexia. Before Madison went to school, she used to be really happy. However, after she enrolled in school, she believed she was dumb and couldn't learn. No one understood why she had trouble learning. It wasn't until the third grade when she was properly diagnosed that Madison felt some relief. Madison was extremely self-conscious. She worked hard to prove to her parents, peers, and teachers that she was "normal."

This is waht a dyslexic person otfen hßs to dael with just to raed a dook

Dyslexia was a genetic impact for Madison. With dyslexia, she had trouble reading, memorizing, and summarizing stories. Madison could hardly breathe as Miss Vone began teaching. Her hands were clammy, and she felt like her body was frozen and rooted in her chair. Even though Madison was 15 years old, she still feared she would be made to feel dumb again just as the kids had made her feel many years ago. They had taunted her for not being able to read. "Madison," she heard Ms. Vone's voice in the distance as it interrupted her troubled thoughts. "Yes," whispered Madison as she fumbled with her pencil. "Madison, can you read paragraph one of page 260?" asked Ms. Vone. After a long pause, Madison responded, "I'm not feeling well. May I go see the nurse?"

We Can Read!

{Laughter}

I must be dumb!

JUDGMENT

Pain

Genetic Impact
Inherited Trait

5. Madison felt that she had been judged in the past because of her disability. She compared herself to others and felt vastly inadequate.

Madison first experienced this negative judgment over nine years ago. Why does this feeling remain so strong for her?

_____

6. What can Madison do to face her fear of being taunted?

_____

7. Do you think Madison judges herself? What could Madison do to build her self-confidence?

_____

8. Circle the emotions you think Madison may be feeling.

DEPRESSION NOSTAGLIA HOPELESSNESS ANXIETY FRUSTRATION FEAR ANGER

Rejection

Why don't you do something with that hair?

And, what's the thick make-up all about?

I'm so ugly. I wish I wasn't here. No one likes me.

REJECTION

Pain

Physical Impact
Injury

Haley remembered when life was good. She used to be a popular girl in middle school. She made good grades and excelled in sports. One day she was with a friend at a party around a bonfire. Someone threw a can into the fire, and it exploded. The shrapnel from the explosion hit her in the face. She had second degree burns. Haley never recovered from the physical and emotional scars. As she got older and in high school, it seemed to get worse. Haley wore heavy make-up to try to cover the scars. She wore her hair down around her face in an attempt to hide the ugliness she felt.

Julia was a popular girl who made good grades and excelled in sports. However, Julia was mean-spirited. She always had something nasty to say to Haley. Whenever Haley spotted Julia or her "girls," she would melt into a doorway or get out of Julia's way as fast as possible. Haley hated to come to school. Many days she missed school in order to keep out of Julia's path. Haley's consistent low grades added to her misery. Haley stayed off of social media to avoid having to see how different she was compared to others. She didn't want to risk being made fun of to the whole world. Haley not only felt different and unpopular, but she seemed powerless. Haley was a victim of bullying.

9.   What might Haley turn to or do out of despair that would make her situation worse?

_____

10. Haley felt isolated. Isolation occurs when we remove ourselves away from others, usually to avoid pain. What does Haley need to help her life take a turn for a positive future? How can she make it happen?

_____

LESSON ELEVEN

EFFECTS FROM THE IMPACTS OF LIFE

ABOUT ANGER

"INABILITY TO COPE" SYMPTOMS

WHEN "PERFECT" GOES WRONG

REVIEW – Fill in the Blanks

- The feelings of _____ and _____ often precede the feeling of anger.
- Our heart functions as our _____ brain.
- Our brain functions as our _____ brain.

EFFECTS FROM THE IMPACTS OF LIFE

An **effect** is an unplanned outcome in our life that is a result of an event. An **event** is something that happens to trigger the life impact. Each of our characters in the short stories experienced negative effects as a result of an event. Mrs. Larson's car accident was the event that triggered the effect of depression and anxiety that Mr. Larson and Zach experienced. Examples of negative effects that young people may experience as a result of life's impacts can be: poor school attendance, high conflict, low grades, and physical symptoms which require visits to the health nurse. Reflecting on our characters, answer the following questions relating to the events and the effects of each scenario.

1. Was it Haley's fault that her face was burned? How did the burning event affect her life?

_____

2. Madison's didn't realize for a while that she had been born with a learning disability. How did the diagnosis (event) affect her life? Was it for the positive or the negative?

_____

3. Andrew's stepfather abused him, made him feel threatened and afraid, and caused him to worry about his mother. This is a reoccurring event. What can he do to lessen the negative effects on his life?

_____

4. Zach's mother was hit by a drunk driver. This event affected Zach as he experienced depression and anxiety. What positive thing can he do to offset the negative effects of this event?

_____

Forgiveness

Forgiveness as a conscious, deliberate decision to release feelings of resentment or vengeance toward a person or group who has harmed you, regardless of whether they actually deserve your forgiveness. When we forgive someone, we don't have to agree with them or continue a relationship with them. Forgiveness is a method to help ourselves to ease the pain we feel from the behavior of others toward us.

5. List the person(s) that our characters might consider forgiving in order to help themselves recover more rapidly from the life impact they have experienced.

Character	Haley	Madison	Andrew	Zach
Person(s) to Forgive				

ABOUT ANGER

All of our characters thus far have had to deal with the strong emotion of anger. When anger is felt for long periods of time it can be harmful. But, you may say, "Our characters didn't hurt themselves or others." While it may be true that they didn't physically hurt themselves or others, they may have unknowingly **psychologically** hurt themselves or others.

There are two types of anger: fleeting and deep-seated. An example of fleeting anger is when an authority figure gives you an ultimatum, "Clean your room, or stay home from the party." This ultimatum may make you angry, but most likely it is justified. While we may think the ultimatum is unfair, we don't necessarily feel that the person is being unfair. Therefore, for a 'fleeting" moment, we get angered. The moment may last for a little while, but it is temporary. After the room is cleaned, and you attend the party, you forget about the emotion, thus there are no harmful effects.

However, when we have anger that is a result of a dart to our heart (such as harm, judgment, or rejection), it can become a "deep-seated" anger. This happens when the dart remains lodged in our heart. Memories of the incident will cause us to wince in pain, as if someone is twisting the dart. Negative reactions to the pain can cause harm physically, verbally, emotionally, or mentally to ourselves or others.

As you see in the chart below, anger is usually a **secondary** emotion. Before we feel deep-seated anger, we probably feel another emotion first, such as depression or anxiety. In our examples, depression or anxiety would be the **primary** emotion. There is an **escalation** of emotions to get to the anger stage. This escalation can happen in an instant or over time.

In the cases that we have reviewed, the characters' depression or anxiety were effects from an event which triggered a life impact. Our characters most likely wished they had things back the way they were. They experienced the feeling of being a victim of something out of their control.

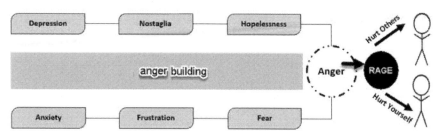

They may have felt frustrated with their situation. They may have experienced hopelessness. They may have been afraid to ask others for what they needed.

Our characters experienced life as unfair putting them on the path to feeling **deep-seated** anger. This may result in them hurting themselves or others as their anger builds. There is a risk they will become like the people who hurt them. Their anger may remain deep-seated putting themselves at the most risk.

"INABILITY TO COPE" SYMPTOMS

 Once we experience deep-seated anger, it becomes more than just another emotion. It becomes a snare around our painful heart where it may restrict us from fulfilling our purposes in life. The pain becomes buried in the snare of anger. The anger becomes prominent and stronger as we experience new darts or triggers. Deep-seated anger will likely affect our physical and mental health. The more layers of the snare, the more intense the "inability to cope" symptoms may become. The "inability to cope" symptoms listed below may be red flags of a heart snared in anger.

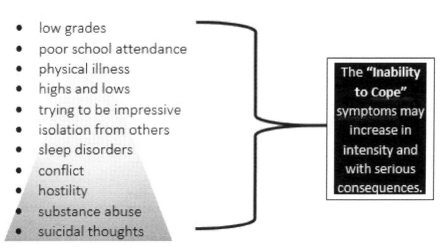

- low grades
- poor school attendance
- physical illness
- highs and lows
- trying to be impressive
- isolation from others
- sleep disorders
- conflict
- hostility
- substance abuse
- suicidal thoughts

The "Inability to Cope" symptoms may increase in intensity and with serious consequences.

The inability to cope symptoms may at first appear to not affect us. For example, our rational brain will tell us that "many students receive low grades", and "many students have poor attendance." When we have low grades or poor attendance at school or work, we lose our ability to cope and be productive. These rational thoughts justify our actions in an attempt to make ourselves feel better. When we are no longer productive or cannot cope, we must closely examine ourselves. How frequent are our symptoms? Have our symptoms increased in intensity? What is the cause of our symptoms? Are we **angry**? Are we **depressed**? Are we **anxious**? Where are we on the path to anger? <u>The "inability to cope" symptoms are not the root problem, but rather indicators that we must identify the cause.</u>

6. Reflect on our characters. List below at least one "inability to cope" symptoms exhibited.

Character	Inability to Cope Symptoms
Zach	
Andrew	
Madison	
Haley	

WHEN "PERFECT" GOES WRONG

Brandon had the perfect home, the perfect parents, and the perfect life. He lived in an elite neighborhood, and his dad was an important person in the community. From the time Brandon started school he had many friends, was the favorite student, and his grades were at the top of the class. He was the star in every sport and competition. He was well-liked and enjoyed his popularity. Brandon's best friend from childhood, Destiny, was always there as his sidekick.

During the summer prior to Brandon's entry into high school, his world fell apart. Suddenly it wasn't cool to be the best athlete and to have the highest grades. A lot of Brandon's friends were turning to alcohol and elite drugs. They were pressuring him to buy illegal substances from them and for them. They wanted Brandon to use his influence and money to sponsor weekend parties. Destiny, his best friend, continually encouraged Brandon to turn away. Additionally, his parents had hopes and dreams for him to be a doctor. He had a reputation of perfection to maintain.

However, it seemed that Brandon couldn't escape. Kids from both social sides, rich and poor, were pushing him to change his way of life. After school one day, Brandon got jumped by the school punk, Ryan. Ryan was smacking his chewing gum, and had his heavily made up girlfriend, Victoria, by his side. Ryan grabbed Brandon by the shirt collar. Brandon could feel Ryan's big cold bling-rings against his neck. "I want you to work with me, Dude!" hissed Ryan. "You got something I want, and I got something your friends want, and soon you will want what I have." "W-w-what is that," stammered Brandon? "You got the bucks, and I got the feel-good stuff", Ryan said. Ryan loosen his grip just a little while Victoria looked in both directions to make sure no one was watching. Brandon's eyes were wide with fear. "What's it going to be rich boy?" Ryan poked. "You coming to my side, or are you ready to deal with the consequences?"

7. Write the rest of the story. What does Brandon do? Does he provide money for his classmates to have parties? Does he participate? How does he react? What is his final outcome?

_____

8. While Brandon's home environment was "perfect," it made him a prime target for an "imperfect" environmental impact when he lost his status. Suppose Brandon continued with his perfect life on the surface, but he gives money to Ryan to buy alcohol and drugs for his friends. Later he begins to participate in the parties where he joins others by partaking of alcohol and drugs. What inability to cope symptoms might Ryan experience? List them in the order of intensity on the triangle with the most intense at the bottom.

9. Why might Brandon decide to start participating in the parties?

_____

LESSON TWELVE

EMOTION MATCH

THE FORCE IS SHAPED WITHIN YOU

FEELINGS TO FORCE FLOW

REVIEW -Fill in the Blanks

- An _____ is a unplanned outcome that is a result of an _____.
- There are two types of anger: _____ and _____ - _____ .
- Having the "_____" symptoms may be red flags of a heart snared in anger.

EMOTION MATCH

Let's review the seven emotions from the diagram we have been studying. The seven emotions are: Depression, Nostalgia, Hopelessness, Anxiety, Frustration, Fear, and Anger.

1. Demonstrate your knowledge. Match the definition below with the emotion.

_____ Depression	A. Apprehension caused by the belief that something or someone may cause you pain or be a threat.
_____ Nostalgia	
_____ Hopelessness	B. Longing for the way things were in the past.
_____ Anxiety	C. Annoyance due to the inability to change or achieve something.
_____ Frustration	
_____ Fear	D. Despair or complete loss.
_____ Anger	E. Extreme sadness.
	F. Strong displeasure.
	G. Worry or uncertainty.

THE FORCE IS SHAPED WITHIN YOU

Force equals strength, energy, or power. The impacts we experience in life produce forces within us. We have been studying how the emotions listed above may result from life impacts, triggered by events with negative effects. Remember, the impacts we have in life may be from a genetic trait as an inherited trait or learned behavior from our experiences. They may be from a physical injury, psychological abuse or loss, as a result of our environment.

When we experience an impact, it is as if a dart goes to our heart causing us to feel a strong emotion. The emotion in our heart sends a signal to our mind where we justify what we are feeling. Our mind constructs thoughts to support what we feel. The thoughts are a result of what we are experiencing with our five senses or what we have stored in memory. Our thoughts cause our body to internally respond. Our internal body may go into overdrive mode and function wildly. Examples of internal responses are: confusion, a racing heart, tight chest, upset stomach, or tense muscles.

The internal response of our body causes an external physical response. The physical response may include: crying, inability to sleep, change in breathing, saggy posture, sweaty palms, flushed face, or perspiring. The physical responses cause a force within you to spring into motion, to fight or run away (fight or flight). The force is like the power when we plug into an electrical outlet. We become "charged." The force produces energy, power, and strength. The force is behind our urge to fight or flight. Sometimes the urge to fight or flight is suppressed until a later time. The force boosts your spirit. Our spirit is either positive or negative. It is either good or bad for ourselves and those around us. Our spirit is often referred to as our character. The Feelings to Force Flow is represented in the graphic below.

FEELINGS TO FORCE FLOW

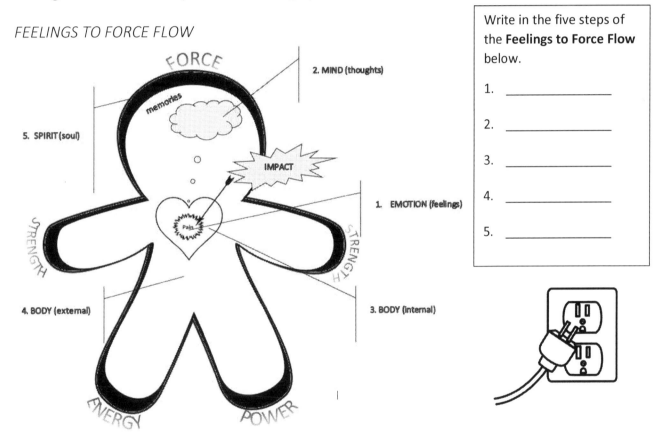

Write in the five steps of the **Feelings to Force Flow** below.

1. _____

2. _____

3. _____

4. _____

5. _____

2. Let's chart the Feelings to Force Flow based on Andrew's story in Lesson Ten. Reread the story. Fill in the blanks in each row in the chart below to show Andrew's response for the components of the Feelings to Force Flow that he experienced due to his psychological impact of abuse and his environmental impact of the loss of safety.

Component	Response
Emotions (feelings)	Anxiety/Fear/Anger/Depression/ _____
Five Senses	Saw menacing stepfather/Smelled alcohol/Felt pain in leg/Heard _____
Memories	Stepfather hitting _____
Mind (thoughts)	"Oh how I hate him!" "If he hits my mother, I'm _____ !"
Body (internal)	Tight Shoulders/Pain in _____
Body (external)	Jumped/Grip Glass/Sweaty palms/Sigh of _____ ,/Hung _____
Force	Fight or Flight?
Spirit Effect	Negative flow for himself – fighting, low _____ Negative flow for others – _____ with others

3. How do Andrew's thoughts (mind) justify what he feels in his heart (emotions)?

_____

4. Our external and internal responses are connected. For example, what internal body response was connected to the external "sigh of relief?" _____

5. Focus on an impact in your life resulting from your genetics, experiences, a physical injury, psychological trauma, or a loss in your environment that caused you to feel a strong emotion(s). How old were you when you experienced your impact? _____

6. Refer to the list of emotions below. Identify the emotion(s) you felt as a result of your impact. Put a check by each emotion that you felt.

Emotions List

Anger	Hatred	Amazement	Suspicion
Depression	Sadness	Anguish	Wariness
Fear	Scorn	Annoyance	Agitation
Frustration	Elation	Confidence	Curiosity
Happiness	Jealousy	Confusion	Embarrassment
Paranoia	Rage	Defeat	Guilt
Satisfaction	Unease	Defensiveness	Hopefulness
Anxiety	Worry	Denial	Loneliness
Regret	Adoration	Desire	Nervousness
Resignation	Conflicted	Disbelief	Relief
Shame	Hurt	Disgust	Skepticism
Contempt	Love	Envy	Uncertainty
Determination	Overwhelmed	Impatience	Amusement
Disappointment	Peacefulness	Insecurity	Anticipation
Dread	Resentment	Irritation	Desperation
Excitement	Smugness	Pride	Doubt
Gratitude	Terror	Remorse	Eagerness

There are many negative impacts in life. Research suggests that every day the average person experiences about 20,000 moments. A **moment** is defined as the few seconds our brain needs to record an experience. An impact can happen in a moment or over a span of time. These moments are either positive, negative, or neutral. Seldom do we remember neutral moments, usually just the positive and negative ones.

7. On a separate sheet of paper, describe a personal experience. Identify in your story something that made you feel a strong **negative** emotion. State "I felt _____ when _____". Incorporate the Emotions List above. Recall any **memories** triggered by the experience. Write about any **thoughts** you had to support how you felt. Describe how your **body** felt **internally** and **externally**. What **force** was activated as a result of your **experience**? Did you want to **fight** or **flight**? How was your spirit (character) affected?

8. Repeat Number 6 above, only this time write a short story where you experienced where you felt a strong **positive** emotion. Incorporate the emotions that you felt using the Emotion List above. Recall any **memories** that were triggered by the impact. Write about any **thoughts** you had to support how you felt. Describe how your **body** felt **internally** and **externally**. What **force** was activated as a result of your **experience**? How was your spirit affected?

9. Review your two stories. Place a check by the emotions in the list above that you identified in your writings. Place one check by each emotion for every time you identified it in your writings. For example, if you identified anger two times, then place two checks by the word, Anger.

10. Make a list of your emotions below which you identified in both of your stories. Rank the emotions by the intensity of your feelings. For example, if you felt anger the strongest, then put anger on the number one line.

   1._____
   2._____
   3._____
   4._____
   5._____
   6._____
   7._____
   8._____
   9._____
   10._____

10. Did you have more negative emotions or more positive emotions on your list?

   NEGATIVE   POSTIVE

11. Do you think you could forgive the person(s) who have caused you harm?

   YES   NO

LESSON THIRTEEN

OUR SENSE CONTROL

LEARNING FROM FAILURES

BUILDING RESILIENCE

REVIEW – Fill in the Blanks

- Force equals strength, energy, or _____.
- Our spirit, just like the electrical outlet has either a _____. or _____. flow.
- An impact can happen in a _____. or over a _____. of time.

OUR SENSE CONTROL

Now that you are aware of how emotions are triggered first in our heart, then in our mind, it may be easier to identify why you feel the way you do. You should better understand your body's reactions and your words and actions.

Our five senses play a big role in how impactful the INPUT of the darts of judgment, rejection, pain, harm and other hurts are to our heart. When these darts come our way, experienced through our senses, we form a memory.

The five senses regulate the intensity of emotions. The pain of the dart can cause us to feel emotions such as: depression, anxiety, nostalgia, frustration, hopelessness, and fear. The information collected through the five senses can trigger a memory or cause a new thought. Our thoughts affect our bodies internally and externally. We produce an OUTPUT which is words, actions, and spirit.

Input affects Output. What we take in affects what we put out. Look at the drawing on the next page. Notice how the possibility of impacts are all around us. There is constant danger of darts hitting our hearts. The darts may be real or perceived from a memory. The darts or even the fear of darts can cause negative emotions in our heart. Our heart then sends justifying thoughts to our minds. This produces a physical response in our bodies and affects our reaction and spirit. What can we do?

In the last lesson, you combated the negative story with a positive story. The possibility exists to cancel a negative experience with a positive one. Research shows that we need multiple positives to cancel a negative, maybe as many as four positives to one negative (4:1).

1. Using colored pencils or crayons, in the next graphic color the impact indicator (judgment, pain, harm, rejection) that has had a strong intensity in your life.
2. Color the internal body arrows (arguing, flight, fight, avoidance, anger) to show how you mostly responded.
3. Color the words listed in the heart corresponding to the type of pain that the impact caused.
4. Color the thought bubble corresponding to the quantity of your thoughts consumed by the impact. How much of the pain consumes your thoughts?

5. Which of the five senses reminds you of your painful impact - seeing, hearing, smelling, tasting, or feeling?

_____

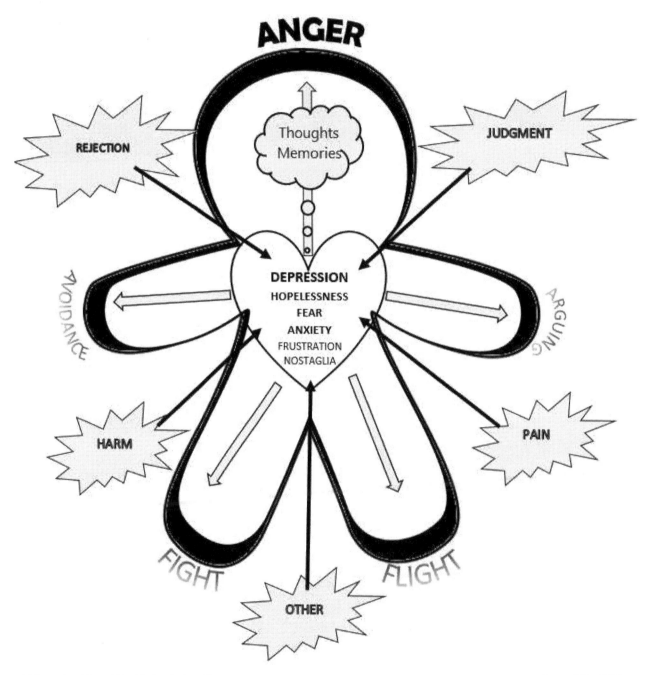

LEARNING FROM FAILURES

Sometimes our failures are considered a negative impact. Failure may be a result of what we allowed to influence us in our environment. Are you someone who can learn from failure? Have you ever combated the negative by turning your failure into flair? Can you think of a time when something caused you pain, and you took the pain and turned it into success? Maybe you helped yourself or others from what you learned.

6. Describe a time when you failed. Did you learn from the failure? Did you turn your failure into success? If you did, describe the success. If not, describe how you could have turned it into a success if the situation was repeated.

_____

_____

BUILDING RESILIENCE

Resilience is the ability to function despite adversity or stress. It is being able to bounce back from life's negative impacts and cope with challenges. It involves being able to handle stress positively. In this part of the lesson, we will learn ways to build resilience to turn a negative into a positive.

7. Circle the answer that best describes you. There are no right or wrong answers.

1)	If I am worried, I can talk to a friend or relative about my problem.	Yes	No
2)	Faith is an important part of my life.	Yes	No
3)	A long hot bath is relaxing to me.	Yes	No
4)	I love me.	Yes	No
5)	I exercise for at least 30 minutes on a regular basis (three times a week or more).	Yes	No
6)	There is an elderly person in my life whom I respect greatly.	Yes	No
7)	I like to learn new things.	Yes	No
8)	I am thankful for many things.	Yes	No
9)	I take short mini-walks every day.	Yes	No
10)	I am connected to a faith-based organization on a regular basis.	Yes	No
11)	I love (or would like) to travel and experience new things.	Yes	No
12)	I eat healthy foods (fruits, vegetables, nuts, etc.) daily.	Yes	No
13)	I have friends or family who are incarcerated.	Yes	No

14) I know what I want to do or be five (5) years from now. Yes No

15) If today doesn't work out, things will be better tomorrow. Yes No

16) When I do a task, I usually finish it on time. Yes No

17) I like to give (time, talent, or treasure) to other people. Yes No

18) I feel lonely on a frequent basis. Yes No

19) I like making new friends. Yes No

20) When something bothers me, it plays over and over in my mind. Yes No

21) I see my mistakes as learning opportunities. Yes No

22) I am a volunteer for a cause that I believe in. Yes No

23) If I start reading a book, I never finish it. Yes No

24) Sometimes I feel pain, but I can't pinpoint where it is specifically on my body. Yes No

25) I frequently have regular quiet time alone. Yes No

8. Complete the tables below to calculate your resilience factors.

Factor	Direction	Sub-Totals	Total
1	Add one (1) point for every YES answer for the following questions: 1, 6, 11, 19.		
2	Add one (1) point if you answered NO to question 13.		
Connections	Add the Sub-Total numbers for Rows 1 and 2 (1 + 2).		

Factor	Direction	Sub-Totals	Total
3	Add one (1) point for every YES answer for the following questions: 4, 8, 15.		
4	Add one (1) point for every NO answer for questions 18 and 20.		
Emotions	Add the Sub-Total numbers for Rows 3 and 4 (3 + 4).		

Factor	Direction	Sub-Totals	Total
5	Add one (1) point for every YES answer for the following questions: 3, 5, 9, 12.		
6	Add one (1) point if you answered NO to question 24.		
Body	Add the Sub-Total numbers for Rows 5 and 6 (5 + 6).		

Factor	Direction	Sub-Totals	Total
7	Add one (1) point for every YES answer for the following questions: 7, 14, 21.		
8	Add one (1) point for every NO answer for questions 16 and 23.		
Mind	Add the Sub-Total numbers for Rows 7 and 8 (7 + 8).		

Factor	Direction		Sub-Total	Total
Spirit	Add one (1) point for every YES answer for the following questions: 2, 10, 17, 22, 25.			

Resilience factors are: Connections, Emotions, Body, Mind, and Spirit. Together these are the building blocks for our **strength, energy,** and **power.** Having strong resilience factors helps a person maintain the whole being.

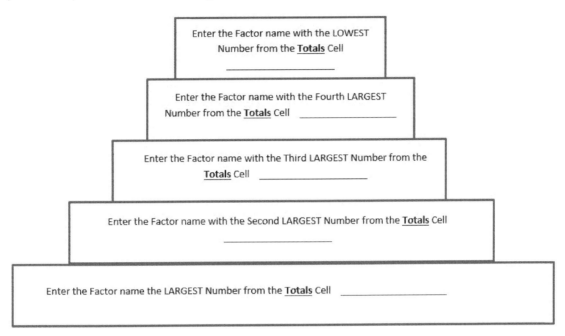

Enter the Factor name with the LOWEST Number from the **Totals** Cell
_____

Enter the Factor name with the Fourth LARGEST Number from the **Totals** Cell _____

Enter the Factor name with the Third LARGEST Number from the **Totals** Cell _____

Enter the Factor name with the Second LARGEST Number from the **Totals** Cell
_____

Enter the Factor name the LARGEST Number from the **Totals** Cell _____

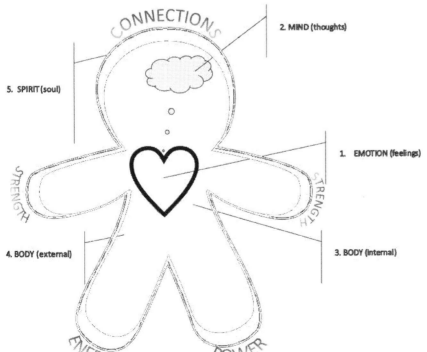

CONNECTIONS

5. SPIRIT (soul)

2. MIND (thoughts)

1. EMOTION (feelings)

STRENGTH

STRENGTH

4. BODY (external)

3. BODY (internal)

ENERGY

POWER

5. Color the strongest part of you:

- Outer Edge for **Connections**
- Heart for **Emotions**
- Body for **Body**
- Thought Bubble for **Mind**
- Outer Shadow of Body for **Spirit**

LESSON FOURTEEN

ASSESSING RESILIENCE

ASSESSING RESILIENCE

Resilience factors that we can strengthen are: Connections, Emotions, Mind, Body, and Spirit. Building resilience involves:

- Connections: connecting through caring relationships;
- Emotions: being aware of your emotions;
- Mind: keeping your mind actively learning something you are interested in;
- Body: staying physically fit; and,
- Spirit: realizing that you have a purpose in life and the power to pursue it.

<u>Connections</u>

Connections to people in our environment can help stabilize us after negative impacts. Others can give us insight which may help us mitigate situations during negative impacts. Connections can provide a strong positive influence to canceling out negative factors.

In an earlier lesson we learned about the important roles in our lives of family, friends, peers, and others. They are our connections. Our connections can be individuals or groups.

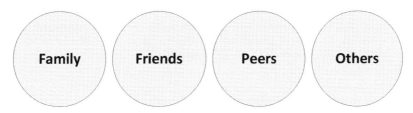

1. Check below the connections that have had a positive impact on you. Check all that apply. If you choose "Other", please specify in the blank.

   a. _____ Teachers
   b. _____ Grandparents
   c. _____ Elderly Person
   d. _____ Pastor
   e. _____ Friend's Parents
   f. _____ Club
   g. _____ Organized Group (Youth, Sports, Support, etc.)
   h. _____ Friend
   i. _____ Family Member
   j. _____ Other _____

2. What could you do to help a friend who may feel disconnected?

Emotions

Our emotions are at the "heart" of a complex system. The heart holds the feelings that make our Emotion Meter move. Emotions are the compass pointing to the effects of an impact. We cannot change how we feel. But once we are aware of our feelings and can identify them we can better predict what may come next in the Feelings to Force Flow. Learning to manage our reaction is key to good mental health. It is important to boost our confidence by building ourselves up and by being around others who can encourage positive responses.

3. Check below the things you do to keep your heart healthy. Check all that apply. If you choose "Other", please specify in the blank.

    a. _____   Be grateful for something every day
    b. _____   Seek to make new friends
    c. _____   Have a pet
    d. _____   Be aware of your feelings
    e. _____   Identify your emotions
    f. _____   Love yourself
    g. _____   Journal
    h. _____   Plan something you enjoy
    i. _____   Are aware what your five senses are experiencing (mindfulness)
    j. _____   Play an instrument
    k. _____   Regularly reconnect with old friends
    l. _____   Forgive easily
    m. _____   Other _____

4. What can you do in the near future to touch a friend's heart?

    _____

Mind

Our minds can swirl with many thoughts. Research says we can have about 70,000 thoughts a day compared to our 20,000 experiences, defined as moments. That's over three thoughts for each moment! We can be up and down, swing low, swing high, and move from positive to negative all within a few seconds. Our mind battles between what is truth versus what we believe to be true. Our truth is our perception from our mind's eye. It is important to fill our minds with things that will help us grow intellectually and mature.

5. Check below the things that fill your mind. Check all that apply. If you choose "Other", please specify in the blank.

a. _____ Assessment of real truth about situations
b. _____ Learning from failure
c. _____ Past successes
d. _____ Dreams of new successes
e. _____ Education
f. _____ New topics not previously studied
g. _____ Short Term Goals
h. _____ Long Term Goals
i. _____ Hobbies
j. _____ Reading
k. _____ Libraries or Museums
l. _____ Writing
m. _____ Other _____

6. What can you do for a friend to help them switch from a negative outlook to being positive?
_____

Body

We have learned that mental health affects our physical well-being, and our physical health affects our mental health. One way to build resilience is to keep your physical body healthy. Making your heart beat fast and sweating due to physical exercise is a positive impact on your body as opposed to being in an environment where your fast heart rate is controlled by your thoughts. Keeping our physical bodies in check helps us to maintain a pleasant temperament.

7. Check below the ways you take care of your physical body. Check all that apply. If you choose "Other", please specify in the blank.

a. _____ Exercise for 30 minutes at least three times a week
b. _____ Eat healthy foods every day
c. _____ Get at least 8 hours of sleep most nights
d. _____ Play sports
e. _____ Take short mini-walks throughout the day
f. _____ Drink at least 8 glasses of water a day
g. _____ Avoid caffeine
h. _____ Avoid sugar
i. _____ Avoid junk food
j. _____ Other _____

8. What could you do to encourage a friend to be more physically fit?
_____

Spirit

Our spirit is the power inside us. It is what drives us to be and do. It is who we are. Our spirit resonates with others and ourselves. We can build up or tear down others and ourselves. Our spirit may be referred to as our soul or presence. It is our heart, mind, and body all bundled in one. Our spirit may live on forever as an influence on others. For example, if someone close to you dies, their spirit may live on through you as you carry out their hopes and dreams or do things to make them proud. Our spirit is noticeable when we enter a room. Do we want to be there? Are we friendly? Are we shy? Are we engaged and connected with others? You have the power WITHIN you (heart, mind, body) to strengthen your spirit. You have the power to live out your PURPOSE in life. The power comes from your environment.

9. Check below indicating what powers your presence. Check all that apply. If you choose "Other", please specify in the blank.

    a. _____ Volunteer time
    b. _____ Spend time with those in need
    c. _____ Mediate or pray
    d. _____ Listen to music that makes your happy
    e. _____ Be a part of a faith-based organization
    f. _____ Spend time with positive people who encourage you
    g. _____ Learn inspiring quotes
    h. _____ Mediate on accomplishments
    i. _____ Speak positive sayings
    j. _____ Other _____

10. What could you do to help transform a friend's spirit from a negative to a positive?

_____

11. From your previous Resilience Factor rating, enter your lowest and highest Resilience Factors in the chart below.

12. Find the section in this lesson that corresponds with your highest Resilience Factor. In the chart below, list what makes you strong.

13. Find the section in this lesson that corresponds with your lowest Resilience Factor. In the chart below, list the things you plan to do to improve your weakest factor.

How I plan to improve my
lowest Resilience Factor:

What makes me strong in my
highest Resilience Factor:

_____

_____

_____

MY LOWEST RESILIENCE FACTOR IS:
_____

_____

_____

MY HIGHEST RESILIENCE FACTOR IS:
_____

14. What can you do to help a friend who has a low Resilience Factor in an area where you have a high Resilience Factor?

_____

But I don't tell you this.
    I don't dare.
        I'm afraid to.
I'm afraid you'll think less of me, that you'll laugh
    and your laugh would kill me.
I'm afraid that deep-down I'm nothing,
        that I'm just no good
            and you will see this and reject me.

So I play my game, my desperate, pretending game
With a facade of assurance without,
And a trembling child within.
So begins the parade of masks,

The glittering but empty parade of masks,
    and my life becomes a front.
I idly chatter to you in suave tones of surface talk.
I tell you everything that's nothing
    and nothing of what's everything,
            of what's crying within me.
So when I'm going through my routine
    do not be fooled by what I'm saying
Please listen carefully and try to hear
    what I'm not saying
Hear what I'd like to say

It will not be easy for you,
    long felt inadequacies make my defenses strong.
The nearer you approach me
    the blinder I may strike back.
Despite what books say of men, I am irrational;
I fight against the very thing that I cry out for.
    you wonder who I am
        you shouldn't
        for I am everyman
        and everywoman
        who wears a mask.
Don't be fooled by me.
At least not by the face I wear. -- unknown

Will you be able to see behind someone else's mask? Will you be able to assess the heart, mind, body responses, and spirit of another to interpret what is behind the mask?

In the poem above:

20. Underline the words, "your laugh would kill me."

21. What type of impact would the laugh be? (genetics, experiences, physical defects, psychological trauma, or environmental loss)

_____

22. Find the words, "a trembling child within." Which resilience factor is affected? (connections, emotions, mind, body, or spirit)

_____

24. With a crayon, circle the words "what's crying within me" of the poem.

25. Color where "crying within" is happening on the graphic.

26. Circle "Hear what I'd like to say".

27. Why can't the author say it? What part of the graphic is taking over?

_____

28. Underline the words, "I may strike back."

29. Which emotion is felt? _____

LESSON FIFTEEN

THE REST OF THE STORY

REVIEW

This lesson is a positive example of a negative situation based on the concepts you have learned. After finishing this lesson, you will have successfully completed the *Behind the Mask: Dealing With Anger, Grief, and Rejection* course.

You have learned the Protection Mask is used when we are afraid of harm, judgment, rejection, or pain. You understand how you are connected to the power roles such as family, friends, peers, and others. You realize that we all have human needs, and that it is acceptable to ask others to help you meet those needs. You understand the differences we may have in perception and beliefs. You learned about the impacts of life and how you can be affected by genetics, experiences, physical defects, psychological trauma, and environmental loss. You have learned about mental and physical health. Remember, the response and recovery to the impacts of life may incite depression and anxiety and may lead to anger.

You also learned:

- that while you may experience hardships and failures, you have power and purpose.
- how to be aware of your own senses, emotions, thoughts, body responses, and reactions.
- ways to build resilience and how to identify critical areas that bring empowerment.

Read the following story. When you are finished, be prepared to identify what the students did to build resilience in the following areas:

- Giving Back to their Community
- Being Productive
- Finding their Purpose
- Learning to Cope and Build Resilience
  - Socially
  - Intellectually
  - Emotionally
  - Physically
  - Spiritually

THE REST OF THE STORY

It was the first day of the new school year. Zach was a senior and eager to complete his last year of high school. The past two years had been hard after the loss of his mother, but Zach was learning ways to cope. While Zach knew his loss was permanent, he had redirected his attention to finishing his high school education well. It is what he believed his mother would have wanted. He felt his mother's spirit was with him, and he wanted to honor her memory.

Zach also planned to honor his mother in a special way. He developed the idea to launch a "Scholars Against Substance Abuse" (SASA) club. He hoped the club would gain popularity and become a national agenda. Zach had learned that the teenager who hit and killed his mother was a substance user. Zach knew his service agenda would not be accepted by all, but if it saved the life of one other person, it would be worth it.

Zach had been regularly seeing a counselor to help him through the grief process. He didn't know, if he would ever fully accept the accident, but he knew he had to move on and make his parents proud.

Zach and his father were working on strengthening their relationship. They regularly played basketball together. Jacob often joined them. Jacob and Zach were best buddies. Jacob had been a friend to Zach through the worst time in his life. Jacob's mother also assisted. She stepped in to help fill the void Zach felt.

Jacob had his own issues. His father and mother had divorced. His father moved away, and Jacob only heard from him occasionally. Jacob learned through a family member that his father had been incarcerated on a drug-related charge. Jacob found comfort in having Zach as his friend. It was nice to have someone to ride bikes with and hang with at the mall. Jacob did not want to follow in his father's footsteps. If he ever had children, Jacob vowed he would never abandon them. Jacob agreed to help Zach with the SASA campaign. Together made a great team, each having a unique purpose while serving the community.

Zach and Jacob worked over the summer to get the campaign plan approved by the local school board. They set goals to teach others about substance abuse. They titled the goals CAR after Zach's mother's "car" accident. The goals were:

- Combat the lure of substance abuse

- Awareness of the short-term and long-term effects of substance abuse

- Response to substance abuse for yourself and others

Zach and Jacob led an assembly at school outlining the CAR goals. They collected student responses electronically via social media. An overwhelming number of students anonymously asked for help for themselves or a loved one. Students who wanted more information could request a private meeting with a counselor. Andrew responded to their call. Andrew knew he needed to reach out for help for his mother and himself. Andrew and his mom were experiencing abuse as a result of his stepfather's substance abuse. The counselor was able to help Andrew and his mom get professional help. She also worked to help Andrew improve his grades. Andrew was encouraged to join the band, as he loved to play the drums. While things were not perfect, Andrew felt more positive than he had in a long time.

Madison approached Zach and Jacob. She had an interest in promoting an anti-bullying campaign. After being bullied because of her dyslexia, she felt empowered to help others who had been bullied. Zach and Jacob referred Madison to the proper school officials to seek approval. Madison thought it would be helpful to team up with a friend. She asked Haley. Together they soon had a large following. A teacher, Ms. Opal, agreed to be their sponsor. Soon, Brandon joined the team and was able to help with fundraise for the promotion. Madison, Haley, and Brandon were soon teaching others how to stand up for themselves. They learned how to respond to others, who belittled them or tried to control them. The students were learning how to deal with their emotions through a network of support from each other. They empowered themselves by building confidence through new personal connections. Haley found a doctor who was able to minimize her facial scars. Madison researched the newest technology to learn what she could do to counteract her struggle with reading. Brandon understoond he didn't have to fear the orders from other kids.

The students held after school meetings. Usually, the meetings were held at Madison's home. During the meetings the students displayed their close connection, as they greeted each other with a fist bump. They gave reports, journaled their progress, and memorized positive quotes. But the highlight of each meeting was playing with Ginger, Madison's golden retriever. Ginger was a part of the team! Woof! The students who had once felt alone and rejected by others now helped each other. They were friends, to whom they felt connected. The students were on their way to fulfilling their purpose in life.

1. Describe two things the students gave back to their community.

_____

2. What did the students do to show they were productive?

_____

3. Describe three coping methods the students used to help them build resiliency.

_____

_____

4. Select one of the students. On a separate sheet of paper, describe what you think might be their destination in life.

POSSIBLE ANSWERS

We say "Possible Answers" because there could a good argument for a different answer!

Lesson 1

Your Answers

Lesson 2

Review
conceals, disguises
outward, inward
self protection

4. D farthest from Star A;
C next farthest; B closest

Lesson 3

Review
play, actors
power, friend
self protection

Lesson 4

Review
self protection
two, more
permanent, temporary

3. Mr. Larson: Angry
    "You could have been in an
    accident! You are grounded
    for a month!"
    Shouting, Lunging, Stare

    Zach: Arguing
    "You don't listen to me like Mom
    did! I am a careful driver!"
    Ran, Slammed door,

4. Safety and Security, Sense of
    Belonging, Self-Esteem
7. accept

5. Arguing, stomach growling; Mr. Larson
    lunge forward; burnt toast, gum; cold stair
    railing, shivering, empty stomach
6,. Avoidance, nothing, left scene
7. Fight
8. Run Away
9. Run Away

Lesson 5

Review

thrive, survive
Protection Mask, "I'm afraid"
threat
Flight, Fight

7. Losing his son
8. Losing his father
9. Avoidance
10. Avoidance
11. Rejection
12. Harm/Rejection
13. Running Away

Lesson 6

Review

Perception, emotions
belief
truth, facts

3. surprised/shocked
4. guilt
5. sadness
6. anger

Lesson 7

Review

unmasking
significant, longer
trigger

1. Learned
2. Green eyes – Inherited
   Freckles – Inherited
   Juggling – Learned
   Rolling Your Tongue – Inherited
   Riding a Bicycle – Learned
4. Anger

Mr. Larson: Genetics: Anxiety;
Environmental: Loss;
Psychological: Overwhelmed
Psychological: Worry about son

Zach: Genetics: Depression
Experience: Anxiety
Environmental Loss
Psychological: Overwhelmed
Psychological: Worry about dad

Lesson 8

Review

genetically, experience, observation
physical, psychological, environmental

8. potential, cope, work, contribution

Lesson 9

Review

response, recovery, physical, well-being

3. Mr. Larson: Sadness of Loss; long term
    Zach: Sadness of Loss; long term
    Mr. Larson: Worry about losing son
    Zach: Worry about losing father

Lesson 10

Review

physical, mental, depression, anxiety,
depression, anxiety

Lesson 11

Review

depression, anxiety, emotional, rational

Lesson 12

Review

effect, event
fleeting, deep-seated
inability-to-cope

1. E, B, D, G, C, A, F
2. Guilt, voice barked into cellphone,
    mother, "gonna punch his face,"
    leg, relief, fight, grades, fighting,
    shoulders relaxed, his leg being hurt

Lesson 13

Review

power, positive, negative, moment, span

REFERENCES

References confirm experiences of survivor and are not meant to be necessarily medically proven.

http://www.merriam-webster.com/dictionary/mask
https://en.wikipedia.org/wiki/Masking_(personality)
http://www.community4me.com/maskexercise2.html
http://blogs.psychcentral.com/emotionally-sensitive/2012/01/wearing-masks/
https://www.bing.com/search?q=acceptance+meaning&form=EDGNTC&qs=DA&cvid=641b450e32274c17882f3be7f5fa4a13&pq=acceptance%20meaning
http://www.inc.com/kevin-daum/define-your-personal-core-values-5-steps.html
http://www.thebridgemaker.com/what-are-your-values-the-most-important-values-to-live-by/
https://www.bing.com/search?q=maslow+hierarchy+of+needs&form=EDGNTC&qs=LS&cvid=0cf3de2471d64b2ab790b86b4aaec529&pq=maslow%20h&cc=US&setlang=en-US
https://www.heartmath.org/research/science-of-the-heart/heart-brain-communication/
http://www.entelechyjournal.com/robinsonwilson.htm
http://faculty.virginia.edu/perlab/pdf/ZadraCloreEmotPercept.pdf
https://en.wikipedia.org/wiki/Belief
https://en.wikipedia.org/wiki/Perception
http://www.merriam-webster.com/dictionary/belief
http://www.news-medical.net/news/20100319/Six-basic-human-emotions-universally-recognized-other-positive-emotions-culturally-specific.aspx
http://www.medicinenet.com/mental_illness/article.htm
http://www.livestrong.com/article/562015-do-children-inherit-their-parents-personalities/
http://education.seattlepi.com/example-learned-trait-4334.html
https://www.psychologytoday.com/blog/embracing-the-dark-side/200811/depression-and-its-metaphors
http://www.who.int/features/factfiles/mental_health/en/
https://www.nami.org/Learn-More/Mental-Health-Conditions
https://www.stopbullying.gov/kids/facts/index.html
http://www.gallup.com/businessjournal/12916/Big-Impact-Small-Interactions.aspx
http://www.apa.org/helpcenter/stress-body.aspx
http://www.sermonsearch.com/sermon-illustrations/7450/negatives-outweigh-positives/
https://www.reference.com/world-view/many-thoughts-per-minute-cb7fcf22ebbf8466

Made in the USA
Columbia, SC
03 August 2018